All Scripture references taken from the KJV of the Holy Bible, unless otherwise indicated.

STRUCTURE: ***Why Order Protects What God Blesses***

by Dr. Marlene Miles

Freshwater Press 2026

Freshwaterpress9@gmail.com

ISBN: 978-1-971933-49-8

Paperback Version

Table of Contents

STRUCTURE

Why Order Protects What God Blesses

When you have no Structure,

the enemy doesn't have to look

for a way to attack.

WHY MONEY DISAPPEARS

People care about money.

They may not say it out loud in spiritual settings. They may soften the language and talk about “provision,” “blessing,” or “financial stability,” but the truth is simple: money affects nearly every part of daily life.

Money determines whether bills are paid. Money determines whether stress enters a household. Money determines whether opportunities can be pursued or must be declined.

So, when money repeatedly disappears from a person’s life, the question eventually rises:

Why?

Many people assume the answer is simple. They believe they do not have money because they have not yet earned enough of it. “If I could just make more money, everything would be fine.” But experience tells a different story.

There are people who make very little money and manage to live with surprising stability. There are also people who make enormous amounts of money and seem to lose it just as quickly as it arrives.

The difference is rarely income alone. The difference is Structure. Money does not remain where Structure does not exist. This is one of the most uncomfortable truths about finances, because it shifts the problem away from external circumstances and toward internal systems.

People often imagine that the solution to financial problems is simply more money. But if money alone solved financial problems, then every person who received a raise, an inheritance, or a windfall would remain permanently secure.

Yet that rarely happens.

Lottery winners frequently lose everything within a few years. Professional athletes and some celebrities who earn millions sometimes end their careers bankrupt. Business owners can generate enormous revenue and still find themselves drowning in debt. We've seen rich doctors, poor doctors, rich lawyers, poor lawyers, rich dads and poor dads. It runs the gamut.

The problem was not the amount of money that entered their lives. The problem was the structure that was supposed to hold it. Money behaves in a predictable way. It flows toward systems that can govern it and away from systems that cannot.

Where Structure exists, money tends to remain and multiply. Where Structure does not exist, money leaks away.

Sometimes it leaks through poor decisions. Sometimes it leaks through disorder. Sometimes it leaks through people who exploit the lack of boundaries. sometimes it leaks through forces the Bible describes in vivid language.

Scripture speaks about devourers that consume resources, wasters that destroy what has been built, swallowers that absorb everything they touch, emptiers that drain what once seemed abundant, and scatterers that disperse what once appeared secure. These are evil forces that slowly drain strength, joy, or bank accounts in maybe not so obvious ways. Some of their tactics are constant crises, disorganization, and unmanaged obligations.

These patterns are familiar to many people even if they have never used those exact words.

Money arrives. Then something happens. An unexpected expense appears. A bad decision is made. An opportunity is missed. A relationship becomes costly. A plan falls apart. Suddenly the money is gone.

To someone experiencing this repeatedly, it can feel like an attack. But the deeper issue can be far simpler. When there is no structure, the enemy does not have to search for a way to attack. The system is already open. Imagine a house with no doors. No windows. No roof. Rain falls, and the house fills with water. Wind blows, and everything inside is exposed. If thieves arrive, they do not need to break in. There is nothing to break. Everything is already accessible.

A house built this way is not attacked because it is especially valuable. It is attacked because it is especially vulnerable. Many financial lives are structured in exactly this way. Money enters, but there are no walls to contain it.

There are no boundaries governing how it is spent. There is no system guiding how it is saved. There is no discipline determining what should be refused.

So, the money comes and goes as freely as the weather. Over time, a pattern forms. People begin to believe that money simply "doesn't stay" with them. As self-fulfilling prophecies go, what people believe and what they say, often eventually create the reality of their lives. Their money does not disappear randomly. Money reveals Structure. Money is not God, but it can act as a revealer of secrets—follow the money. Where Structure exists, money tends to remain. Where Structure does not exist, money becomes temporary.

The blessing of the Lord maketh rich, and he addeth no sorrow with it. (Proverbs 10:22)

Blessing does not remove the need for Structure. Blessing brings increase. God has given us power to get wealth. But where is the wherewithal to keep it? Structure determines whether that increase can remain. Without Structure, even blessing can become overwhelming. What enters a life faster than it can be governed eventually creates pressure. That pressure exposes weaknesses in the system.

A person gets a blessing. With or without Structure, there goes a signal out into the spirit realm: This person just got a blessing. The devil is a thief. Thieves steal. They will steal pretty much anything—everything. The devil has sophisticated thieves and an orchestrated thievery system.

STRUCTURE

The Invisible Architecture

The devil sends a barrage of stuff at you. Suddenly there's a storm coming against whatever Structure is in place in a person's life. In a storm, there's thunder, lightning, hurricane, tornado, monsoon, hail. What will keep the driving rain out of your house?

Structure determines what a life can hold. Structure is intangible. It cannot always be seen directly. Yet Structure determines whether anything in life can stand, remain, or multiply.

Without it, resources scatter. With it, resources remain. Understanding that difference is the first step toward building something strong enough to withstand what life eventually brings.

Most of the forces that determine the outcome of a life are invisible. You cannot see governance. You cannot see discipline. You cannot see Wisdom. You cannot see order. Yet these invisible structures around a life determine whether a life remains stable or collapses under pressure.

When people experience loss, chaos, or repeated setbacks, they often blame circumstances, other people, or spiritual attacks. But many times, the real issue is simpler and harder to recognize:

The Structure that should hold their life together was never built. Structure is the invisible architecture of a life. It determines what enters. It determines what remains. It determines what survives. Where Structure exists, pressure can be endured, opportunity can be governed, and increase can be preserved. Where Structure is absent, even blessings leak away.

Money flows where there is Structure. God looks on the Structure of a man's life to see how that man would handle blessings. Not only the Structure God has set up for that man; but also how that man has used what God has given him and structured his own life by his own acts and choices. God is our Ever-Present Help, we are not out here all on our own, but we do have free will and we make our own choices day by day. Structure determines what survives. Everything else supports that idea.

When money repeatedly disappears from a person's life, the question eventually rises:

Why?

Many answers can be offered. Some blame the economy. Some blame employers. Some blame other people. Some blame bad luck. Some blame spiritual attack. Sometimes those factors are real. Circumstances do matter. External forces can influence a person's financial life.

But there is another possibility that is less often discussed. Sometimes money disappears because the Structure that should hold it does not exist.

Money does not simply enter a life and remain there automatically. Like water poured into a container, money remains only when something exists to hold it. If the container has holes, the water leaks away. If the container has cracks, the water slowly escapes. If the container does not exist at all, the water spreads everywhere and disappears. The same principle applies to money.

Money requires Structure.

Without Structure, money behaves like water poured onto open ground. It runs in every direction and eventually vanishes. This is why some people can earn large amounts of money and still have nothing left. It is also why other people with modest incomes manage to maintain stability and progress over time.

The difference is not always the amount of money entering their lives. Often, the difference is the Structure surrounding it.

Structure is not always visible. You cannot see discipline the way you see a building. You cannot see governance the way you see a wall. You cannot see priorities the way you see a roof. Yet these invisible structures determine whether money remains or disappears. When these structures exist, money has a place to remain. When they do not exist, money eventually leaves.

Many people assume the solution to financial instability is simply more money. We are taught that in movies and stories. Even well-meaning stories where money needs to be raised to save the farm, the church, the business, or for grandma's surgery. In those stories we are led to believe that the needy are needy because they never had; but did they? What is their structure like if they have one? No one looks at that because it doesn't make for good cinema. But we don't live in the movies; we live in real life.

More money does not fix structural problems. In fact, more money often exposes them. When the Structure of a life is weak, an increase of money does not create stability. It simply increases the speed at which money flows in and out.

The problem is not always that money never came. Sometimes the problem is that nothing was built to hold it. This book is about the Structures that allow money—and many other forms of blessing—to remain.

Money is not preserved by desire; money is preserved by Structure.

Many enemies of structure will be named in this book. They are Devourers, which are things that eat resources slowly. Neglect, poor stewardship, and bad habits. The Wasters are things that destroy what has been built. Examples: impulsive decisions. pride-driven choices, and emotional spending. The Swallowers are things that consume everything that enters. Examples: addiction, uncontrolled appetite, status chasing. The Scatterers are things that cause loss through lack of focus. Examples distraction, comparison, competition, and lack of priorities. The Emptiers which we have already mentioned are also culprits. Some of these things are natural; some are spiritual. Most often though, that which is spiritual brings on what is seen in the natural.

We will do well to remember this: When the house is built properly, many would-be assailants lose their power and many attacks are rendered harmless.

THE HOUSE WITH NO WALLS

Many people believe they are under constant attack; and perhaps they are. I would not venture to say a person who is under spiritual or financial attack is not because I am not in their life. So, this person might pray against enemies, rebuke devourers, and ask God to remove obstacles from their lives. They feel as though something is always working against them, always stealing from them, always breaking what they try to build. That could be the case, especially if they sense it. That could be the case by no fault or cause of their own; these kinds of things can be inherited, generational, or familial. If you look into the patterns of your family and everyone is experiencing the same thing no matter how hard they work, try, get schooling, or start businesses, you're not imagining that there's an evil pattern.

Sometimes the problem is the absence of Structure. I'm not saying that you don't have Structure: this lack of Structure way of living or of life could have been passed down to you or modeled before you by your parents and their parents before them.

If a person doesn't have Structure, maybe they learned that system from their parents and foreparrents. The Structure of which we speak is compared to natural structures but we are talking about spiritual structure. Spiritual structure is established to protect from and ward off spiritual attack.

The unbuilt house with nothing protective or shielding in place. If bad weather comes, the house is exposed. Thieves can come like looters in a riot, the place is wide open. There is nothing to break.

Many lives are built this way.

Without realizing it, people remove the very Structure s that protect what God places in their lives. They remove discipline. They remove boundaries. They remove governance. They remove order. Then they wonder why everything leaks away.

When a house has no roof, rain does not have to search for a way in. When a house has no doors, intruders do not have to force entry. If a life has no Structure, the enemy does not need to look for an opening. The house is already open.

Structure is protection. Structure is what allows a house to hold what falls upon it. Rain is not the enemy of the house. Rain is provision. But provision cannot remain where there is nothing built to hold it. In the same way, opportunities, money, favor, responsibility, and blessing often come into people's lives like rain. The problem is not that rain never falls. The problem is that many houses are not built to hold it.

God does not only release blessing; He also teaches people how to build structures which we will compare to houses that can keep it.

Structure is intangible. The most powerful Structures in life are not physical. They are invisible systems that govern visible outcomes. Structure is not the building. Structure is the system that holds the building together. It is the framework. You cannot always see it directly, but you always see its effects.

For example, Structure exists in thinking, discipline, priorities, boundaries. Structure is seen in habits, governance, Wisdom, and order. These things are invisible, yet they control everything that is visible.

Structure is intangible, but its absence is obvious.

Most people try to fix visible problems without addressing the invisible Structures that created them. You cannot see Structure directly, but you can always see what it produces.

Authority governs a territory. Structure governs what happens inside that territory. There are three layers of Structure. Internal Structure is the structure of the mind and character: discipline, Wisdom, restraint, and maturity. Life Structure is the structure of daily living such as routines, priorities, stewardship, and boundaries. Spiritual structure is alignment with God's order. It is Covenant, obedience, humility, and discernment. Structure is the invisible architecture of a life.

Blessings can arrive suddenly, but Structure must be built and ready for those blessings. Therefore, a man should spend his time correcting or perfecting the Structures of his life and not only asking repeatedly for blessings from God.

THE HOUSE WITH NO ROOF

Think of that same building or house that we have mentioned; it has no doors. It has No windows and no roof. The frame of the house exists. The outline of the structure can be seen. But the parts that provide protection are missing. If rain falls, the house fills with water and possibly ruins it even though the water will eventually flow out.

If wind blows, everything inside is exposed.

If thieves arrive, they do not need tools or force to enter. They simply walk inside. Prayer is not optional for a Christian. It is known in witchcraft circles that a house without prayer or proper spiritual covering has *no roof.* Any witch flying over can just drop in, almost literally.

Nothing stops them.

A house built this way does not fail because the weather is unusually harsh. It fails because the structure never protected what was inside it. That house was barely standing in the spirit, if at all.

Many lives are built in exactly the same way. Money enters the house, but there are no doors controlling where it goes. Resources pass through the house, but there are no walls establishing boundaries. Pressure arrives, but there is no roof protecting the system beneath it. When loss follows, people often blame the storm. But the storm did not create the problem; the storm only revealed it.

Worse, the lack of a structure actually invited intruders. In the natural that would be true as it is also true spiritually speaking.

A house with no roof will fill with water every time it rains or anything undesirable that wants to drop in, can. A house with no doors will allow anyone to enter. A house with no windows cannot see what approaches.

The same principle applies to a life. When structure is missing, vulnerability becomes constant. In that condition, the enemy does not need to search for a clever way to attack. The system is already open. Wide open.

Instead of asking only, "Why did this happen to me?" the wiser question becomes: What part of my Structure was missing?

Storms of life will come; we can't just wish them away. Pressure comes. Opportunity comes. Increase comes. Good or bad, these are forces, and when they arrive, the strength of the Structure determines what stays, what goes, and what survives and lasts.

By proper spiritual covering and prayer you state what goes and what stays. If you are 'prayed up,' you have pre-stated it before anything every came your way. You have a roof over your head. You have a roof over your house, over your Structure.

EXPOSURE

Money disappears for many reasons, but one of the most overlooked causes is exposure. Exposure happens when something valuable exists inside a system that has not been properly secured. The value may be real, but the protection is weak or missing.

People understand this principle in the physical world. No one leaves the doors of their home open at night and then acts surprised if strangers walk inside. No one stores valuables in an unlocked building and then wonders how they disappeared.

Protection requires Structure.

In many areas of life, people live as if Structure does not matter. They assume that good intentions will protect them. They assume that hard work alone will protect them. They assume that sincerity will somehow keep destructive forces away.

Yet life does not operate that way.

Where Structure is weak, exposure increases.

And where exposure increases, loss eventually follows.

This principle applies to many areas of life, but money reveals it very quickly. Resources move through systems constantly. If those systems are poorly structured, the resources escape almost as quickly as they arrive.

Understanding exposure takes wisdom. Once a person understands exposure, they can begin to ask a more important question:

Where is my Structure *weak?*

The next chapter explores that question through a simple image that makes the problem impossible to ignore.

THE STRUCTURE OF A LIFE

Structure is rarely dramatic. It does not announce itself loudly. It does not attract attention the way sudden success or sudden failure does. In fact, Structure often appears ordinary. It is built quietly through small decisions repeated consistently over time. Yet these quiet systems determine whether a life can withstand the forces that eventually arrive.

Many people imagine Structure as something rigid or restrictive. They associate it with limitation rather than freedom. True Structure does the opposite. Structure creates stability.

It allows resources to remain where they belong. It allows decisions to be made with clarity rather than panic. It allows opportunities to be evaluated rather than chased blindly. Without Structure, life becomes reactive. Every pressure creates urgency. Every opportunity creates distraction. Every increase creates confusion.

With Structure, life becomes governed. Decisions are made intentionally. Resources are directed wisely. Pressure is managed instead of feared. The strength of a Structure depends on the elements that support it.

Just as a building depends on beams to carry weight, a life depends on certain internal supports that allow it to remain stable. These supports are not always visible, but they determine whether a system holds together when pressure increases.

Five of these supports appear repeatedly in strong, stable lives. They act like beams carrying the weight of the structure. When these beams are strong, the system holds. When they weaken, the system begins to fail.

THE FIRST BEAM: GOVERNANCE

Every Structure begins with governance, which is the ability to rule oneself. It is the capacity to make decisions based on wisdom rather than impulse. It is the discipline to restrain desires when those desires conflict with long-term stability.

Without governance, Structure cannot exist.

Money cannot be managed without governance. Time cannot be used wisely without governance. Opportunities cannot be evaluated properly without governance.

Governance places leadership inside the system.

Instead of reacting to circumstances, the person becomes capable of directing them.

Many people attempt to build financial stability without first establishing governance. They search for better investments, higher income, or clever strategies while leaving the underlying decision-making process unchanged.

But strategies cannot replace governance.

If the person governing the system remains undisciplined, every strategy eventually fails. The first beam of Structure must therefore begin within the individual. Before a person governs resources, they must learn to govern themselves.

THE SECOND BEAM: BOUNDARIES

Boundaries determine what may enter a system. A house with strong walls controls access. Doors allow entry only where permission is granted. Windows allow vision while still maintaining protection. Without boundaries, a Structure cannot remain secure.

In financial life, boundaries determine how money moves. They define limits for spending, commitments, and obligations. Without boundaries, resources move in every direction at once.

Money arrives, but demands quickly follow. Opportunities appear, but they compete with one another. Commitments multiply until they consume every available resource.

Boundaries protect the system from becoming overwhelmed. They ensure that what enters the Structure does so in an ordered way. Many people struggle financially not because money never arrives, but because boundaries never exist.

Without boundaries, the system remains open to every influence that passes through. Open systems rarely remain stable.

THE THIRD BEAM: STEWARDSHIP

Stewardship determines what happens after something enters the Structure.

Resources must be managed.

Money must be directed.
Time must be allocated.
Opportunities must be cultivated carefully.

Stewardship recognizes that resources are not merely possessions but responsibilities.

When something enters a life, stewardship asks:

How should this be used?

How should this be preserved?

How should this be multiplied?

Without stewardship, resources drift toward waste. Small decisions accumulate until the system becomes disordered.

With stewardship, resources serve a purpose. They move intentionally rather than randomly. This is why stewardship often distinguishes people who appear outwardly similar. Two individuals may receive the same opportunity, yet their outcomes differ dramatically because one governs the resource carefully while the other allows it to disperse.

Stewardship protects what governance and boundaries have secured.

THE FOURTH BEAM: DISCERNMENT

Discernment allows a system to recognize danger before damage occurs. Not every opportunity is beneficial. Not every relationship strengthens the system. Not every idea deserves attention.

Discernment evaluates influences before they enter the Structure. It recognizes deception, distraction, and misdirection. It notices patterns that others ignore. It identifies forces that quietly weaken stability.

Without discernment, a person may unintentionally invite destructive influences into their life. Discernment protects the Structure by identifying threats early.

It closes doors before harm enters.

THE FIFTH BEAM: ALIGNMENT

Alignment determines who ultimately governs the Structure. Human wisdom can build systems, but lasting stability requires alignment with God's order. When a life aligns with Divine Wisdom, the Structure gains a foundation deeper than human effort alone.

> The blessing of the Lord maketh rich, and he addeth no sorrow with it. (Proverbs 10:22)

Alignment places the entire Structure under the guidance of God's Wisdom rather than human impulse alone. Without alignment, even well-designed systems can drift.

With alignment, the Structure gains direction, purpose, and protection beyond what human planning can achieve. When these five beams work together, a life gains strength. Governance provides leadership. Boundaries provide protection. Stewardship manages resources. Discernment guards the entrances. Alignment anchors the Structure in God's order.

Together, they form the framework capable of carrying weight. But even strong Structures can fail if weaknesses appear within them.

Before we examine the Biblical picture that illustrates preservation under extreme pressure, we must first understand the hidden fractures that often weaken a system from the inside.

THE 5 PILLARS OF KEEPING MONEY

Pillar 1 — Governance (Rule Yourself First)

Money stays where there is self-governance. Many people think keeping money is about math, but Scripture shows it is first about character and discipline. If you cannot govern your impulses, you cannot govern your resources. Money flows toward governance and runs away from chaos.

Pillar 2 — Structure (Order Holds Provision)

Money requires a Structure to land in. Without Structure money leaks, emergencies multiply, impulse spending increases Haggai 1:6 talks about the bag with holes. Provision without Structure disappears. Increase must land somewhere that can hold it.

Pillar 3 — Stewardship (You Are Managing, Not Owning)

Scripture consistently teaches that we manage what God entrusts. This is seen clearly in the Parable of the Talents in the Gospel of Matthew. The servants were evaluated on how they governed what was entrusted to them.

Money stays longer in the hands of a steward than in the hands of an owner. Another Ownership breeds pride. Stewardship breeds responsibility.

Pillar 4 — Discernment (Recognize the Devourers)

Some loss is natural, but some loss is **systematic**. Through the elite, effective and ancient organization off thieves called: devourers, wasters, swallowers, emptiers, and scatterers

Discernment means recognizing patterns like impulse purchases, comparison spending, competition spending, emotional spending, and pride spending. If you cannot recognize what eats your money, you cannot stop feeding it.

Pillar 5 — Covenant Alignment (Blessing Without Sorrow)

Money is safest when life is aligned with God's order.

The blessing of the Lord makes rich and adds no sorrow with it. (Proverbs 10:22)

When money comes outside of covenant order, stress increases, conflict increases, and sorrow increases. Money gained outside of wisdom usually comes with sorrow attached.

In summary: govern yourself first to establish Structure. Steward what enters your hands and your life. Discern what destroys and always stay aligned with God. When governance, Structure, stewardship, discernment, and covenant alignment are present, you have found the right place for money. In this case, money has somewhere safe to stay. Money is not kept by desire. It is kept by wisdom, governance, and stewardship. It stays where Wisdom lives.

THE HOUSE THAT HOLDS THE BLESSING

Continuing with our example of comparing a person's life to a house structure, Can the house contain or hold onto the blessings, especially when it is money?

Governance (The Foundation)

Governance is the foundation of the house. If the foundation is weak the house shifts, the walls crack, and everything becomes unstable

If the foundation is weak, nothing you build on it will stay stable. If a person cannot govern themselves, no amount of money will stabilize their life.

Structure (The Frame of the House)

Structure is the framework of the house. It gives shape and order. Without a frame, the roof cannot sit. The walls cannot stand. The house collapses. Provision cannot stay where Structure does not exist.

Stewardship (The Roof)

Stewardship is the roof of the house. The roof protects what is inside. If the roof has holes, rain leaks in. Damage spreads. The house deteriorates

You earn wages to put them into a bag with holes. If the roof leaks, it doesn't matter how much rain falls (Haggai):

Discernment (The Doors and Windows)

Discernment is the doors and windows. They control what is allowed in and what is kept out. Without discernment: devourers enter, wasters enter, scatterers enter. If the doors are left open, destruction walks in.

Covenant Alignment (The Owner of the House)

Covenant alignment answers the most important question:

Who owns the house?

When the house belongs to God. His Wisdom governs it. His order protects it. His blessing rests on it.

The blessing of the Lord makes rich and adds no sorrow.
(Proverbs 10:22)

When God governs the house, the blessing can rest there without sorrow. Money is like rain. Rain will fall on many houses. But only the house with a strong foundation, solid structure, a sound roof, guarded doors, and the right owner will keep what falls.

The question is not only whether money comes. The question is whether your house knows how to hold it. Money stays where Wisdom has built a house. The issue is not just whether money comes — it's whether the house is built to keep it.

Where there is no structure, the devil doesn't have to look for a way to attack. No door, no window, no roof — you're an open target. Many attacks succeed not because the enemy is strong, but because structure is missing. Structure is spiritual protection. Where structure exists chaos decreases, devourers lose access, resources remain, peace increases, authority becomes stable. Where structure is missing, attack becomes easy, waste increases, disorder multiplies, and blessings leak away

Spiritual warfare is much easier when the house is built properly. Structure closes doors the enemy hopes you never notice are ajar or even wide open. Order itself is a form of defense. Armies go out to battle in order. They go out in rank and file and by phalanxes. Sometimes your spiritual warfare is not flashy battles--, just order. Setting things in order and maintaining that order is warfare.

ENEMIES EXPLOIT DISORDER

Disorder invites attacks. On deliverance ground it is said that many demons, devils prefer disorder and chaos. They thrive in it and feel comfortable, even invited into that sort of situation. When there is no structure, the enemy does not need to find a door. Disorder opens access through impulsiveness, lack of discipline, unmanaged emotions, and lack of boundaries.

Not all threats to Structure are catastrophic. Most are slow, ordinary, and ignored. But they are still constantly testing and testing, to see how strong or secure a structure is.

PHASE 1 — INVISIBLE & DAILY PRESSURES are the ones people sometimes ignore or underestimate.

1. **Wind** (Pressure & Movement)

- Opinions
- Trends
- Emotional shifts
- Other people's instability

Wind does not break a house immediately. It tests how it is anchored."

2. **Sun** (Exposure & Time)

- Long seasons
- Repetition
- Success without adjustment
- Slow drying out (burnout, overextension)

What blesses you can also wear you down if you are not structured to endure it."

3. **Cold** (Restriction & Tightness)

- Scarcity seasons
- Contraction
- Fear-based decisions
- Withholding instead of stewarding

Cold reveals whether your Structure was built for flow or for fear.

4. **Neglect** (Silence & Delay)

- Not checking systems
- Not maintaining discipline
- Letting small things go

Most structures do not collapse from attack. They collapse from neglect.

PHASE 2 — HIDDEN DAMAGE

Now we move from external to internal threats.

1. **Varmints** (Small Intrusions)

- Leaks
- Bad habits
- Unchecked spending
- "It's just a little" decisions

What is small but consistent will outlast what is large but occasional.

2. **Moisture** (Slow Corruption)

- Emotional reasoning
- Rationalization is compromise

Damage that stays hidden is damage that spreads.

3. **Firc** (Misuse of Power)

- Sudden increase
- Access without discipline
- Opportunity without Structure

Fire is not a problem, until it touches what you don't want burned.

PHASE 3 — VISIBLE STRESS (T*hings start showing*)

8. **Shifting Ground** (Foundation Issues)

- Wrong priorities

- Misaligned values
- Building on unstable thinking

You cannot stabilize a structure built on movement.

9. Weight (Increase)

- More money
- More responsibility
- More access

Increase is not just a reward; it is a weight.

PHASE 4 — FINAL PRESSURES

10. Floods (Overwhelm & Volume)

- Too much at once
- Sudden influx
- No containment system

Floods do not destroy strong structures. They expose weak ones. You are not losing things at random.
You are losing them at the points where your structure cannot hold.

The preceding is the flow of the next 10 chapters as we look at what these things can do to a structure and to a life.

WIND

What Moves Against You First

. Wind is not solid; it has no form, no structure, and no weight you can hold. Yet, it has power and force to move things. Wind does not need to break a Structure to affect it. It only needs to push. Wind tests alignment. It presses against what is already built to see what shifts. A well-anchored structure does not fear wind. It has already accounted for it in its construction.

Wind is constant. Opinions shift. Voices rise. Trends movc. Emotions change. Nothing stays still for long. In matters of money, wind looks like influence. What people say you should do. What others are doing around you. What feels urgent in the moment. What appears attractive but is not anchored.

Wind does not ask you to collapse. It asks you to move slightly. Just enough to adjust, just enough to bend, just enough to reconsider what was already decided. If you are not anchored, you will. Small shifts become new positions and can lean a person toward misalignment with God.

New positions become new patterns. What began as pressure becomes direction.

Wind is not always wrong. But it is not always right.

That is why Structure matters. Without internal order, external movement becomes internal instability. A structure that responds to every wind will not remain stable. You cannot build consistency while adjusting constantly.

Wind reveals what is anchored and what is reactive. If your decisions change with pressure, your Structure is not governing—you are being governed. The issue is not that wind exists, it is that you must have something in place to hold you in place.

You need a fixed standard, a settled decision, and internal order, so when pressure comes, you will not be moved. What moves repeatedly does not hold. Stay anchored in the Lord and His Word so you are not tossed about by winds of doctrine.

SUN

What You Are Exposed To Over Time.

The sun gives light. It gives warmth. It sustains life, well, under normal conditions. We need the sun to live, yet, over time, it also wears things down. Things fade or can over dry or burnout or burn up. What is exposed continuously is affected eventually. The sun does not need force. It has duration. Day after day. Season after season, without interruption.

In Structure, the sun represents long exposure. Not crisis. Not pressure. Just… time. In matters of money, the sun looks like sustained seasons. steady income. ongoing responsibility. Repeated success. Prolonged access. Nothing is wrong. Everything is working.

That is where the testing begins. Because what is continuous can become casual. Attention relaxes. Discipline softens. Precision fades. Not because anything failed—but because nothing forced correction.

The sun reveals what can endure without urgency.

Many structures are built to respond to pressure. Few are built to withstand ease. When things are working, maintenance is often ignored. Systems are not checked. Patterns are not examined. Decisions are no longer intentional. Because it feels safe.

But exposure is still happening.

Heat dries.

Over time, flexibility can become brittleness. Strength can become fatigue. Consistency can become assumption. What is not refreshed becomes worn. The danger of the sun is not what it does quickly. It is what it does slowly while everything appears fine.

Some losses do not come from crisis. They come from overexposure without maintenance. If you continued, but did not adjust, the structure may begin to fail. If you sustained but you did not renew, what held for a while begins to weaken.

Duration without correction leads to decline. The sun is not the problem. Unattended exposure is.

What you live in continuously will shape what you become—whether you examine it or not.

TIME / PRESSURE

What Accumulates

Pressure is not always immediate. Sometimes it builds. Not in moments, but in layers. One decision. Then another. Then another. Nothing seems significant on its own. But pressure does not measure single moments. It measures accumulation. In Structure, time reveals what has been repeated.

Not what was done once— but what has been done consistently. In matters of money, pressure is cumulative. repeated overspending, repeated neglect, repeated misalignment, repeated access without governance.

None of these collapse a structure immediately. But they do not disappear. They stack. Pressure builds quietly. What was manageable at first becomes weight over time. What was small at first becomes pattern, then pattern becomes structure. This is why some outcomes feel sudden. Collapse is visible all at once— but the pressure was not. Time exposes what has been growing or building beneath the surface.

It is not what you intended. What you repeated.

You do not experience the result of one decision. You experience the result of many decisions compounded. Pressure does not ask if you are ready. It simply reflects what has been accumulated. If discipline has been repeated, stability will be present.

If neglect has been repeated, instability will be present. Time does not create outcomes. It reveals them. Because what you build slowly you will face eventually. There is no urgency in accumulation. That is why it is often ignored. But what is ignored does not disappear.

It develops. And when it reaches capacity, it expresses. Pressure is not punishment. It is exposure. It reveals the total weight of what has been added over time. You are not facing one moment. You are facing everything that has been building.

These together: the Sun and its prolonged exposure (ease, success, continuation), and Time/Pressure accumulating (what builds beneath awareness) can be very damaging.

Nothing is leaving anyone's life randomly. What remains is not determined by desire. It is determined by Structure. There are forces that act on everything you receive—some visible, some subtle, some cumulative.

If your Structure cannot withstand them, what comes will not stay. This book is not about chasing more. It is about understanding why what you have does, or does not remain, so when you do receive more, you can keep it, steward it, and manage it well.

COLD

When Things Stop Flowing

Cold does not press like wind. It does not spread like moisture. It does not consume like fire. It's kind of sneaky. It shows up and it restricts.

Cold tightens what once moved freely. It slows. It hardens. It limits. Flow becomes effort. Ease becomes resistance. In Structure, cold is not destruction; it is contraction. In matters of money, cold looks like scarcity. Reduced flow delayed opportunities. It looks like tighter margins, and increased caution. Cold exposes relationships to provision.

Some respond with discipline, others respond with fear. Cold does not create character; it reveals it. What you believe about supply becomes visible when flow decreases. Some grip. Some withdraw. Some panic. Some freeze. Decisions change under cold. What was once generous becomes guarded. What was once clear becomes uncertain. What was once structured becomes reactive. Cold tests consistency. It asks, *Will you remain ordered when there is less?*

It is easy to appear structured when there is plenty. It is easy to feel stable when nothing is threatened. But cold removes excess. It reveals what was unnecessary, what was unsustainable, and what was never structured to begin with And then there is this: "I would that thou wert cold or hot…" Because instability is not only in extremes.

It is indecision. Lukewarm Structure is unstable Structure. Not fully disciplined. Not fully surrendered. Not fully governed. Just enough effort to appear functional. Not enough order to remain consistent. Cold forces clarity. It removes the illusion of abundance and exposes the reality of Structure.

What remains when things tighten is what was truly established. Cold is not the enemy. It is a revealer. It shows whether your Structure depends on flow or is built to function without it. Because what only works when things are easy is not Structure.

If your order disappears when things tighten, it was never established—it was supported. These two together: Wind and its external influence that tries to move you along with cold that restricts flow will test your consistency. So, now what happens when flow changes? It's not just what you do when things are good, it is also what I become when things change. Wind and cold tested movement and scarcity—now we deal with the next pressures to Structure.

VARMINTS

Small Things That Stay

Varmints do not arrive as a threat. They arrive small. Quiet. Unnoticed. They do not announce entry. They find openings. A structure is not only tested by what strikes it. It is tested by what enters it.

Varmints do not need permission.

They need access. A gap. A crack. An oversight. Something small left unguarded. What is small is often dismissed. "It's nothing." "It's just a little." "It won't matter." But what is small and repeated is never insignificant. Varmints do not destroy immediately. They settle. They remain. They multiply. They consume slowly.

By the time their presence is obvious, their damage is already established. In matters of money, varmints are patterns. Small, repeated outflows that are never challenged, subscriptions not reviewed, impulse decisions justified, minor losses ignored, or "just this once" repeated. None of these collapse a structure overnight.

That is why they remain. The danger of varmints is not their size. It is their consistency. What you tolerate repeatedly becomes a system. Not because you intended it—but because you allowed it. A house with a small opening will not stay empty. It will be occupied. Not by what you planned— but by what found access.

Most people are not losing money in large, dramatic ways. They are losing it in small, unexamined ways. Daily. Quietly. Consistently.

When loss or a debit is small, it can often be ignored. Because it is ignored, it is repeated. Because it is repeated, it becomes established. Varmints thrive where there is no inspection. No correction. No interruption. In the natural life it is signing up for some service at $5.99 a month and forgetting all about it. Years later, you've spent ***how much?***

You do not remove varmints by wishing they would leave. You remove them by identifying entry points, closing access, interrupting patterns. If the opening remains, the problem remains. This is not about perfection. It is about awareness.

What you refuse to address because it is small will grow large enough to demand attention. Small losses are not harmless. They are indicators. They reveal where access is unguarded, where discipline is absent, where Structure is incomplete. A Structure that cannot manage small intrusions cannot withstand larger pressures. What stays small long enough becomes normal, and what becomes normal is no longer questioned or even noticed.

You are not being drained all at once. You are being diminished in small, permitted ways.

MOISTURE

What Spreads Without Sound

Moisture does not arrive with force. It seeps. It does not break through the structure. It enters it. Gradually. Persistently. Moisture is not immediately destructive. That is why it is dangerous.

In some places, they call it *damp*. It's not flooding. It doesn't cause instant collapse. Just… constant, low-level intrusion. Walls appear intact. Surfaces appear stable.

But inside, something is changing.

Moisture softens what was firm. It weakens what was strong. It distorts what was aligned. It does not announce damage. It spreads it. In matters of money, moisture is internal.

It's not external pressure— but internal compromise.

It looks like quiet rationalization, emotional decision-making, shifting standards. justifying what should be corrected. It sounds like, "It's not that serious." "I deserve this." "It will balance out later."

Moisture changes the structure from within. Not by force, but by influence. What was once firm becomes flexible. What was once clear becomes negotiable. What was once disciplined becomes optional.

Nothing collapses immediately, so it quietly continues. Moisture thrives where there is no ventilation. No correction. No exposure. What is not brought into the open is allowed to remain. What remains will spread. You cannot build strong structure on softened material.

By the time moisture is visible, it is already established. This is why some losses are confusing. Nothing obvious failed. Nothing dramatic happened.

Yet, things no longer hold. Because what was strong was slowly weakened. Moisture does not destroy loudly. It removes strength quietly. What you quietly allow to shift will eventually alter what you are able to sustain.

Damp (England) vs US Equivalent. In the UK, “damp” refers to persistent moisture inside walls/structures that causes mold, rot, staining, and weakening of materials. Types of damp:

- Rising damp → moisture coming up from the ground
- Penetrating damp → water coming through walls
- Condensation damp → buildup from inside (poor ventilation)

In U.S. terms, closest equivalents: moisture damage, mold issues, water intrusion, and hidden rot. Damp implies: *ongoing, subtle, spreading—not dramatic flooding*

NEGLECT

What You Didn't Check

Neglect is quiet. It does not announce itself. It does not demand attention. It does not arrive as a crisis. It waits. Neglect is the absence of inspection. The absence of correction. The absence of maintenance. What is left unattended will not remain neutral. It will drift.

A structure does not fail the day it collapses. It fails in the days it was not examined. The hinge that was never tightened. The leak that was never addressed. The account that was never reviewed. The habit that was never corrected.

None of these are dramatic. That is why they are dangerous. Neglect creates a false sense of stability. Because nothing is visibly wrong, you assume everything is secure. Because nothing has failed yet, you assume nothing will. But neglect is not passive. It is active deterioration. In matters of money, neglect is rarely obvious.

It looks like not tracking where things go, not questioning repeated losses, not reviewing patterns, not adjusting behavior after exposure. It sounds like: "It's fine."

“I’ll check it later.” “It’s not that serious.” Neglect thrives in delay.

In the natural most people do not lose money because of a single event. They lose it because small losses were ignored, repeated patterns were unexamined, discipline was postponed. Loss becomes visible only after neglect has been established. A house that is not maintained does not collapse immediately. It weakens.

Wood softens. Seals break. Edges separate. By the time damage is visible, it has already spread. Neglect is not the absence of effort. It is the absence of governance.

You can be busy and still be neglectful. You can be active and still be unstructured. Because movement is not inspection. Effort is not order. What you refuse to check, you permit to continue. What you permit to continue will eventually establish itself.

What is established will require more to undo than it did to correct. Neglect asks for nothing, until it takes everything.

FIRE

When Increase Arrives

Fire is not always destruction. It is also power. Fire gives access. It expands options. It accelerates movement. It creates opportunity. But fire is not safe by default. It must be contained.

A Structure that cannot govern fire cannot benefit from it.

In matters of money, fire looks like increase. More income. More access. More opportunity. More open doors.

Many people are not destroyed by lack. They are exposed by increase. Because increase does not correct Structure; it reveals it.

If discipline is absent before increase, it will remain absent after. If boundaries are unclear before increase, they will remain unclear after. If access is ungoverned before increase, it will expand after.

Fire magnifies everything it touches. Good Structure becomes more effective, while weak Structure becomes more unstable. This is why some people rise with increase and others unravel under it. Fire requires containment.

Not restriction—but order. Defined boundaries. Clear decisions. Governed access. Without containment, fire spreads. Not because it intends to destroy—but because it is not controlled.

Many losses are not caused by the absence of money. They are caused by the mismanagement of increase. More money does not create discipline. More money requires it. If structure is not strengthened when increase arrives, pressure will follow.

Fire does not adjust to your readiness. It reveals it.

Some people pray for more without preparing for what more demands. When it comes, they experience faster loss, wider exposure, greater instability. Not because increase failed them— but because Structure did not support it.

Fire must be placed. It must be directed. It must be governed. Otherwise, what was meant to build will consume. Increase is not the problem. What you do with it—and what holds it—is.

WEIGHT

Increase Is Not Light

Increase is not a reward. It is a weight. When more comes, more is required. More attention. More discipline. More Structure. What increases is not only what you receive— it is what you must now carry. Many people pray for increase without understanding weight. They ask for more money, more access, more opportunity— without preparing the Structure that must hold it. And when it comes, they celebrate. But they do not adjust.

Weight reveals Structure immediately. What cannot carry begins to strain. What is not reinforced begins to shift. What is unprepared begins to fail. Not because increase is harmful— but because it is heavy.

Money has weight. Not just in amount, but in decisions, responsibilities, access, and expectations. If your structure is unchanged, but your increase grows, the pressure will expose you.

Now consider this Weight is not only what you receive. It is also who you allow. Too many people. Too many opinions. Too many dependencies. Too many hands in what should be governed. Some structures do not fail because of external pressure, they fail because of unauthorized access.

Every person added to your structure adds weight. Their needs, expectations, influence, and their potential disorder. If they are not governed, they do not assist the Structure; they strain it. *Unknown* people are weight. Ungoverned people are weight. Unaligned people are weight.

Access is not neutral. Who you allow near your resources, your decisions, your systems— will either stabilize or destabilize what you are building. Some losses are not financial errors. They are access errors.

A structure that was built to carry one level cannot sustain another without reinforcement, but many try. They increase without restructuring. They expand without strengthening. They add without governing. And then they wonder why it does not hold.

Weight does not apologize. It does not adjust to your readiness. It simply presses. What you call pressure is often capacity being exceeded. Increase requires decisions. Decisions require authority.

Authority requires Structure. If Structure is absent, weight will expose it. Every time.

You are not collapsing because you received too much. You are collapsing because too much was placed on what was never strengthened to carry it.

- Neglect = what you didn’t maintain
- Weight = what you weren’t prepared to carry

SHIFTING GROUND

What You Built On

A structure can be well-built and still fail. Not because of how it was constructed— but because of where it was placed. Ground matters. If the foundation is unstable, everything built on it is at risk--, not immediately. But inevitably. Shifting ground does not always move quickly. Sometimes it settles slowly.

At first, nothing appears wrong. The structure stands. The walls hold. The systems function. But beneath it, something is changing. Pressure reveals it. Time reveals it. Weight reveals it. In matters of money, shifting ground is misalignment.

Building on unstable priorities, unclear values, inconsistent decision-making, external influence instead of internal order. It looks like progress, until it doesn't hold.

You can build income on unstable ground. You can build access on unstable ground. You can build opportunity on unstable ground. But you cannot sustain it there. Because the issue is not what is built. It is what it rests on.

When ground shifts, the structure compensates.

It adjusts. It strains. It redistributes pressure. But compensation is not stability. Eventually cracks appear, alignment is lost, pressure concentrates, and what once held begins to fail. Not because it was weak—but because it was unsupported.

Many people try to reinforce the structure without addressing the ground. They add more effort. More systems. More control. But reinforcement cannot correct misalignment.

You do not fix shifting ground by strengthening what is above it. You correct what is beneath it. Foundation determines sustainability. If your decisions are inconsistent, your outcomes will be unstable.

If your values shift, your Structure will follow. What you build on will determine what you can keep. You are not losing what you built. You are losing what you built on.

These two chapters together: Moisture, which is internal compromise which creates a softening, along with Shifting Ground which leads to foundational misalignment pack a whammy. Together they answer: *Why things stop holding even when nothing obvious broke?*

THREE FLOODS EVERY LIFE WILL FACE

Life does not remain calm forever.

Periods of quiet may last for a time. Systems may appear stable. The weather may seem predictable. But eventually something changes.

Pressure arrives. Sometimes it arrives slowly. Sometimes it arrives suddenly. But eventually every life experiences forces that test whatever Structure exists beneath the surface.

The Bible describes one of the most dramatic examples of this reality in the story of a flood; that is God's flood and we will talk more about that later. For now, know that the enemy typically sends floods in one of three forms. They are designed to:

1. overwhelm
2. increase (mismanaged)
3. pressure / confusion / destabilization

Floods appear in many forms throughout life, not just in ancient times, but even now. Floods represent moments when forces become too large to ignore.

Water that once flowed gently becomes overwhelming. Systems that once seemed stable are suddenly tested. What once appeared secure must now prove whether it can withstand pressure.

Floods reveal Structure.

FLOOD ONE: THE FLOOD OF PRESSURE

The first kind of flood people recognize easily is the flood of pressure.

Pressure arrives in many forms.

Unexpected bills appear. Health problems interrupt normal routines. Relationships break under strain. Plans fail in ways that could not have been predicted.

These moments feel like storms.

The weight of responsibility increases while the margin for error decreases. Decisions that once seemed simple now carry consequences that affect many areas of life.

Pressure reveals the strength of a system very quickly. When pressure enters a life that lacks Structure, panic often follows. Decisions become reactive instead of thoughtful. Resources are spent impulsively. Problems multiply faster than they can be addressed.

But when pressure enters a life supported by strong Structure, the response is very different.

Structure slows panic.

Boundaries remain in place. Disciplines continue operating. Wisdom guides decisions. The pressure may still be real, but the system holds. This is why pressure often reveals more about a person than calm seasons do.

Calm seasons hide weaknesses. Pressure exposes them. Yet pressure is not the only flood that tests Structure.

This is the flood most people think about. The flood of pressure includes crisis, loss, temptation, financial strain, illness, conflict or spiritual attack. When pressure comes, a life without Structure collapses quickly.

Discipline disappears.
Order breaks down.
Emotions take control.

Sometimes the enemy looks to see if you have a sound Structure. If you don't, he doesn't have to do anything to you--, just send a flood.

But when Structure already exists, the pressure hits the Structure rather than the person. Just as the ark protected those inside it, the invisible Structures of a life protect what God has placed within it when the floods of life come.

When pressure arrives, weak systems collapse quickly. Strong systems hold.

Many people think the greatest danger in life is hardship. But hardship is only one kind of flood. There are others. Some floods come through pressure and crisis. Others come through opportunity. Some come through sudden increase. Each of these floods tests the Structure of a life in a different way.

Understanding these floods helps explain why some people remain stable under pressure while others lose what they once possessed. The difference is not always strength. The difference is Structure. Pressure reveals whether an ark has been built.

FLOOD TWO: THE FLOOD OF OPPORTUNITY

Opportunity can destroy a life just as quickly as crisis. When sudden opportunity appears, people are often overwhelmed by it. Another type of flood often arrives when life suddenly becomes easier

Opportunity floods a person's life with money, influence, responsibility, attention, and success. Without Structure, opportunity becomes dangerous. People make impulsive decisions. They expand faster than they can govern. They chase everything instead of stewarding anything.

Many people have been destroyed by opportunity they were not prepared to manage. Opportunity is a flood that can drown an unstructured life. Structure allows a person to govern opportunity rather than be overwhelmed by it.

Opportunity is rarely described as a flood. Most people welcome opportunity with excitement. A door opens. A chance appears. A possibility that once seemed distant suddenly becomes real. Opportunity can feel like a blessing, and often it is. But opportunity carries its own kind of pressure.

Opportunity increases responsibility. It increases decisions. It increases movement within a system that may not be prepared to handle the change. A person who lacks Structure may respond to opportunity with enthusiasm. However, without governance, they may say yes to everything. They expand faster than they can manage. They pursue possibilities without building the systems necessary to sustain them.

What begins as opportunity slowly becomes overwhelm. Projects remain unfinished. Commitments multiply. Resources become scattered. Opportunity, without Structure, becomes another kind of flood. The opportunity itself is not the problem. The system receiving it is.

FLOOD THREE: THE FLOOD OF INCREASE

Increase changes everything. When resources multiply, the Structure that once seemed sufficient suddenly carries far more weight. Money increases. Responsibilities increase. Influence increases. Expectations increase.

Increase magnifies whatever already exists within a system. If discipline exists, increase multiplies stability. If disorder exists, increase multiplies chaos. Many people believe they need more money to solve their problems. Increase without Structure often intensifies those problems rather than solving them. More money increases spending opportunities. More influence increases relational complexity. More responsibility increases pressure on decision-making.

If the underlying Structure has not been strengthened, increase exposes every weakness in the system. This is why some people appear to struggle more after receiving more resources than they did before. The increase revealed structural weaknesses that once remained hidden.

Increase is different from opportunity. Opportunity is a door opening. Increase is a multiplication already happening. Increase floods a life with resources, responsibilities, relationships, and expectations. Without Structure, increase seeps away. Money disappears. Time disappears. Energy disappears.

But when Structure exists, increase becomes multiplication. This principle is seen in the story of the widow and the oil in 2 Kings 4. The oil flowed until the vessels ran out. Increase stopped where capacity ended. Structure creates that capacity.

Understanding these floods leads to an important realization. Floods are not the true enemy. Floods simply reveal whether the Structure of a life has been built to withstand what is coming. And when floods rise high enough, the question eventually becomes unavoidable. What kind of Structure can preserve life when the waters rise? The answer to that question appears in one of the most remarkable stories ever recorded in Scripture.

The Ark as in Noah's Ark that protected him and his family and animals two by two from 40 days and nights of rain and flooding, protects against all three. The ark protects against: Pressure, because it provides strength. Opportunity. because it provides governance especially in the face of increase and great increase, because it provides capacity.

Structure protects a life from three floods: the flood of pressure, the flood of opportunity, and the flood of increase. Many people believe they need protection from hardship. Few realize they also need protection from opportunity and increase. Don't be afraid of opportunity and increase; prepare for it.

Structure does not only protect during storms. Structure also governs success. Without Structure pressure destroys, opportunity overwhelms, increase leaks away. But with Structure, all three types of floods become manageable.

The ark holds. The ark is not just about surviving disaster; it is about surviving life itself.

THE ARK WE MUST BUILD

Every life requires an ark. *Build that ark; go in there, put in everything that you want to multiply. Everything that you do not want to multiply, do not put that in there.* A man who is watching over his family and providing a prayer covering for them is building an ark, whether he realizes it or not.

An ark is not built because life will always be calm. An ark is built because floods come. Floods do not always look the same. In life, people encounter three different kinds of floods, and Structure determines whether those floods destroy them or carry them safely forward.

Some people build an ark; many do not.

Structure is not always visible to others. When someone builds discipline, order, boundaries, and governance into their life, the work often looks unnecessary to people watching from the outside.

In the days of Noah, the ark must have seemed absurd. There was no flood yet. The sky looked normal. Life went on as it always had.

Yet Noah kept building.

He built while others laughed. He built while others doubted. He built while others continued living as if nothing would ever change.

The ark was not built because the flood had arrived. The ark was built because the flood would come.

In the same way, every person must decide whether they will build the invisible Structures of their life discipline, Wisdom, boundaries, governance order. These things often look unnecessary when the weather is calm.

But floods always come. Pressure comes. Loss comes. Temptation comes. Opportunity comes. The question is not whether rain will fall.

The question is whether a Structure exists to preserve what God has placed inside the house. Every person is building something with their life. The only question is this:

Will you stop building when people scoff?

Or will you keep building the Structure that will carry you safely through the flood?

Everyone either builds or neglects an ark — is incredibly powerful because it frames Structure as preparation for inevitable pressure, not just financial management.

This ark you cannot see. Every life has Structure. Some people build it intentionally. Others build it accidentally. Many never realize it exists at all. Yet Structure is always present. It is the invisible architecture beneath every life, holding together what is visible on the surface.

When a life stands strong, Structure is there. When a life collapses under pressure, the absence of Structure is usually close behind.

Structure is not always visible. You cannot always point to it the way you can point to a wall or a roof. But you can always see its effects. You see it in discipline. You see it in boundaries. You see it in Wisdom. You see it in the quiet order of a life that does not easily fall apart when storms arrive.

Structure determines what survives the storms of life, even the long-lasting storms. Even the storms that last 40 days and 40 nights—a lifetime or the better part of one.

Too many people spend their lives trying to fix visible problems without ever addressing the invisible framework beneath them. They try to repair outcomes without rebuilding the Structure that produced those outcomes. They chase more money without building stewardship. They pursue success without establishing governance. They pray for blessing without preparing a **Structure** that can hold it.

Some don't realize that they don't have a Structure. Some don't know that a Structure is needed. Some think that what the world defines as Structure is enough, maybe even aplenty.

So they set out into the world to make their fortune. But when what they receive begins to leak away, they wonder why. Blessing alone does not preserve a life. Having money does not preserve that money, necessarily. Structure does.

Scripture illustrates this principle through one of the most famous structures ever built. In the days of Noah, God instructed Noah to build an ark long before the flood arrived.

To everyone around him, the command must have seemed unnecessary. The sky was clear. The ground was dry. Life appeared normal. Yet Noah kept building. He built while others questioned him. He built while others laughed. He built while others continued living as if nothing would ever change. Noah's ark was not built because the flood had arrived. The ark was built because the flood would come. That ark was more than a boat. It was a structure designed to preserve life when destruction covered the earth. Inside it, life was protected. Outside it, everything was swept away.

In the same way, every person must build what might be called an invisible ark. This ark is not made of wood and pitch. It is built from Wisdom, discipline, boundaries, stewardship, discernment, and alignment with God. These structures form the invisible framework of a life. They determine whether a person can withstand pressure. They determine whether opportunity can be governed wisely. They determine whether increase can multiply instead of disappear.

Without these structures, the floods of life overwhelm people quickly. But with them, a person can endure storms that would otherwise destroy them.

Floods come to every life. Sometimes they come as pressure and hardship. Sometimes they come as opportunity and responsibility. Sometimes they come as increase and blessing. But the question is always the same: *Is there a Structure strong enough to hold what is coming?*

In the Bible God was ever telling man to build things, altars, an ark, the Temple, and even the Ark of the Covenant. God is exact and exacting. Notice though, He always gives instructions.

Understanding the invisible architecture of a life and discovering the beams that strengthen it, the cracks that weaken it, and the Wisdom required to build something as God instructs so that it can endure. The truth is simple; floods will come. But a life built with Structure can carry what the flood brings without being destroyed by it.

Noah and the ark in Genesis preserved life, protected against destruction, carried the future, held what would multiply later. But the ark had to be built before the flood, not during it.

Structure works exactly the same way. Structure preserves resources, protects blessing, keeps destruction outside, carries the future safely. Structure must be built before pressure comes.

Structure is an invisible ark. Before the flood came, the ark had to exist. Before pressure comes into a life, Structure must already be built.

The two main functions of Structure: Keeps In blessing, provision, Wisdom, Peace, and stability. Keeps Out devourers, chaos, destruction, waste, and disorder. That dual function is exactly what an ark does.

People often pray for protection, increase, and preservation, but sometimes the answer God gives is: Build the ark. Build an ark.

Many people pray for God to stop the flood, but God tells them to build the ark. “The ark was not a reaction to the flood. The ark was preparation for it. And the house was preparation for the ark. The assaults of wind, sun, cold, weather, was foreboding of the floods. Have you built your ark? Are you precious to the plan of God? Yes, else you wouldn’t be here.

Structure: the invisible ark that preserves what God Blesses. Structure: Building the Invisible Ark of a Life

Even the Ark of the Covenant functioned similarly to Noah’s Ark – perhaps a forerunner of it. The Ark of the Covenant It was a container of sacred things. It is a place of God's presence, and it is heavily structured and protected because of outside forces that want to invade, spoil, steal, takc, usc or ruin what is inside.

Your ark: to be fully protected from the storms of life, we all build one, or we should. Will we stop when neighbors mock? Or will we keep building the Structure because the floods will come, they will surely come.

THE ARK BEFORE THE FLOOD

Most people do not think about structure until something collapses.

They notice it when money disappears. They notice it when pressure overwhelms them. They notice it when opportunity arrives and everything suddenly feels chaotic. But by the time collapse becomes visible, the problem has usually existed for a long time.

Structure is rarely noticed when it is working properly. Like the beams hidden inside a building, structure quietly carries weight without drawing attention to itself. Yet when those beams are weak or missing, the entire structure eventually fails.

This is true not only for buildings, but for lives.

Every life has an architecture.

Some people build it intentionally. Others allow it to form randomly. But whether it is built carefully or neglected entirely, the Structure of a life determines what it can carry.

In Scripture we find one of the clearest pictures of this principle in the story of **Noah** in **Genesis**. Noah built an ark before the flood came. When Noah began building, the flood had not yet arrived. The skies were clear. Life appeared normal. The work must have seemed strange to those who watched him. Why build such a massive structure when there was no immediate danger?

Yet Noah continued building. He built while others laughed. He built while others ignored him. He built while others continued living as if the future would look exactly like the present. The ark was not built because the flood had arrived. The ark was built because the flood would come.

Every life will face floods. Some floods bring pressure. Some floods bring opportunity. Some floods bring increase. The question is not whether floods will come. The question is whether a structure exists to withstand them.

Structure is the invisible architecture of a life. It governs what enters. It preserves what remains. It protects what must survive. Without structure, blessings leak away. Opportunity overwhelms. Pressure destroys, but when structure exists, the same floods that destroy others can carry a person safely forward.

This book is about understanding the invisible beams that hold a life together, recognizing the cracks that weaken those beams, and allowing the Master Builder to strengthen what must carry the weight of the future, because floods will come. And every person must decide whether they will build the ark before the rain begins.

Structure is intangible. Structure governs outcomes even when it cannot be seen. Floods will come to every life. But the life that builds its Structure with the Master Builder will not collapse.

THE FIVE BEAMS OF THE INVISIBLE ARK

Beam 1 — Governance

Governance is the beam that holds the entire Structure steady. It is the ability to rule yourself. restrain impulses. Make decisions wisely, and submit to discipline. Without governance, everything collapses. The first Structure of a life is self-governance. I am not over-emphasizing it. A person who cannot govern themselves cannot protect what God places in their hands.

Governance stabilizes the ark especially during the flood of pressure.

Beam 2 — Boundaries

Boundaries are the walls and doors of the ark. They determine what enters and what remains outside. Without boundaries, devourers eat, wasters enter, and chaos pervades. Boundaries include relational boundaries, financial boundaries, emotional boundaries, and time boundaries. Boundaries decide what your life will carry and what it will refuse.

Beam 3 — Stewardship

Stewardship governs what happens to resources once they enter the ark. Stewardship includes care, preservation, responsible use, and intentional management. Many people receive blessing but lack stewardship. Stewardship is the beam that prevents increase from leaking away. This beam protects against the flood of increase.

Beam 4 — Discernment

Discernment is the beam that allows a person to recognize threats. Discernment answers questions like: *What is wise? What is a trap? What should be refused? What should be accepted?* Discernment recognizes the enemies already named:

- devourers
- wasters
- swallowers
- emptiers
- scatterers

Discernment closes doors before destruction enters.

Beam 5 — Alignment with God

This beam determines **who governs the ark**.

Alignment means:

- walking in covenant
- submitting to God's Wisdom
- allowing divine order to shape life

Without alignment, the ark may exist but it drifts. When God governs the ark, the blessing can rest inside it.

The Structural Picture

So, the ark holds when these beams exist:

1. **Governance** — rule yourself
2. **Boundaries** — control what enters
3. **Stewardship** — preserve what arrives
4. **Discernment** — recognize threats
5. **Alignment** — submit to God's order

When the beams are strong, the ark holds. When the beams are weak, floods destroy what the ark was meant to preserve. Blessing is not preserved by luck; it is preserved by Structure.

THE SEVEN CRACKS IN THE ARK

There can be subtle weaknesses that may lead to failure.

Jesus, Himself the son of a carpenter, carried beams.

Jesus, raised in the house of Joseph, a carpenter, would have spent years around wood, framing, beams, and structures. And then later, on the way to the crucifixion, Jesus Christ carried the beam of His own Cross. The Son of God literally carried a load-bearing beam.

Before Jesus carried the crossbeam of redemption, He lived in the house of a carpenter, where beams were cut, shaped, and set in place to hold structures together. structure carries weight.

The Seven Cracks in the Ark

If the five beams give the ark strength, the seven cracks explain why structures fail. They are subtle weaknesses that allow the flood to enter. These cracks often appear quietly, long before collapse happens.

Crack 1 — Disorder

Disorder is the absence of intentional structure. Things drift. Responsibilities blur. Priorities disappear. Chaos slowly spreads. Disorder is the silent enemy of preservation. Order at least allows if not brings favorable increase.

Crack 2 — Impulsiveness

Impulsiveness weakens governance. Instead of decisions being guided by wisdom, they are driven by emotion, pressure, excitement, and comparison. Impulsiveness opens the ark to the flood of opportunity. Think, and get wise counsel before making any decisions.

Crack 3 — Pride

Pride convinces a person that structure is unnecessary. It whispers things like, "I can handle this." "I know what I'm doing." "I don't need counsel." Pride removes the supports that keep the ark stable. Pride is the air under self exaltation.

Crack 4 — Covetousness

Covetousness destabilizes contentment. It pushes people to chase what others have rather than steward what they possess. Covetousness fuels comparison, competition, reckless decisions. Covetousness weakens the ark from the inside. Wanting what others have is a sign of ungoverned appetite.

Crack 5 — Lack of Boundaries

Without boundaries, the ark has no sealed doors. Everything enters--, demands, distractions, unhealthy relationships, and unnecessary obligations. A life without boundaries is an ark with open doors. You cannot say yes to everything and every request.

Crack 6 — Neglect

Neglect slowly weakens structure. Small responsibilities ignored today become large problems later. Neglect often appears as procrastination, laziness, and avoidance. Structures collapse quietly under neglect. Pay attention.

Crack 7 — Forgetting God

The most dangerous crack is forgetting who governs the ark. When a person drifts away from alignment with God, Wisdom fades, discernment weakens, and pride grows. The ark begins to drift.

Again, the blessing of the Lord makes rich and adds no sorrow. This is told to us in the Bible because there are blessings or things that seem to be blessings that have sorrow attached to them. Most often those blessings are from the dark kingdom. It doesn't mean that they didn't start out as blessings, but on the back end, when the sorrow is grievous, most will repent of making that deal. Prayerfully it is not too late and they can repent to the Lord, but why risk it?

But thou shalt remember the Lord thy God: for it is he that giveth thee power to get wealth, that he may establish his covenant which he sware unto thy fathers, as it is this day.
(Deuteronomy 8:18)

We all would do well to remember ALL of that verse in Deuteronomy 8:18; the purpose of getting wealth is to that we would remember God and also that He would establish Covenant with us. When the Lord is removed from the center, sorrow eventually enters.

Floods rarely destroy strong structures. Cracks do. The ark does not fail because rain falls. The ark fails because something in its structure was weakened.

THE MASTER BUILDER

The Master Builder chapter is about the role of God in helping rebuild a damaged ark.

Every ark must be built, but who knows how to build one properly? They may sense that something in their life lacks structure. They may see the cracks forming. They may even recognize that floods are coming. But they do not know where to begin. This is where the Master Builder enters the story.

Scripture describes God as a builder and architect.

In Hebrews 11:10, Abraham is said to have looked forward to: "a city which hath foundations, whose builder and maker is God." God does not only create worlds — He designs structures.

He builds lives.

We need a builder. Many people try to repair their lives with effort alone. They attempt discipline without wisdom, boundaries without discernment, OR ambition without alignment. The result is often a house patched together but still unstable.

The Master Builder does something different. He begins with the foundation.

The Builder sees what we cannot. A builder looks at a structure differently than the people living inside it. Where others see a wall, the builder sees the beams, the joints, the stress points, the cracks forming beneath the surface.

God sees the invisible architecture of a life. He knows where the structure is strong, where it is weak, where the ark must be reinforced

The Builder restores Structure. When God rebuilds a life, He restores governance, Wisdom, discipline, boundaries, alignment. Sometimes that rebuilding process feels slow. Sometimes beams must be replaced. Sometimes cracks must be sealed. But when the Master Builder finishes His work, the Structure can carry weight again.

GAINS WITH SORROW

The works of the flesh are not free. They feel immediate. They feel justified. They feel personal.

Cares of this world are either designed or instrumental in taking money and increase and blessings out of the hands of a man. Distraction, disorder, disobedience, wanting to be like everyone else in the world, these are all costly propositions.

Works of the flesh are expensive. They cost money. So, if your soul is not prospered neither will your wallet be. (3 John 2). Each work of the flesh costs something. Even if you don't pursue after the works of the flesh, those who want to take from a man will show up. Whatever a man is enticed into by the dark kingdom, it is set up for that man to lose. NEVER to gain; always to lose.

There are more elite evil agents such as devourers, emptiers, scatterers, wasters, swallowers. That is why the conversation about money must eventually move beyond money itself. Money is rarely the root problem. Money is simply the most visible symptom of something deeper.

The works of the flesh. I propose that they are expensive. they each cost money (or something valuable)

They will be listed and then it will be shown how each could cost money and influence the loss of money. Seriously, what does a person gain from gaining the world, or becoming like the world? What does he gain really, if he loses his soul. Is this not like the 'blessing' that a person thought was a blessing until sorrow followed?

Isn't losing one's soul, certainly sorrow?

Judas gained 30 pieces of silver and thought he had gotten in good with those who wanted to kill Jesus, but didn't Judas then go away sorrowful? Yes, that was that kind of blessing that did not come from the Lord.

The works of the flesh are expensive. They don't just cost spiritually—they drain resources, distort decisions, and dismantle structure.

"What does a person actually gain?"

God made Adam and Eve. Man is made to be a spiritual being.

We don't know how long it took but the serpent worked on them until they because self-aware, so self-aware, flesh aware. Naked and ashamed. Naked (uncovered). Aware – sin guilt. The devil's goal was to turn them into carnal beings. Godly and spiritual beings the devil cannot control. Carnal beings, the devil can run them all day and all night.

Being carnal costs. Yes, it costs spiritually, but it cost in the natural, as well. The first loss in Scripture was not financial—it was the loss of position through disobedience. Just as being in flesh costs money in the natural, a man requires finances for upkeep—a house to live in, food to eat, and clothes to wear is the bare minimum. If carnality is added to that, expenses go though the roof.

Before Abraham and all his wealth, Before Solomon and all his riches, Adam and Eve lost the first empire of the Bible: The Garden of Eden… it doesn't say they owned it, but they had full access to everything in it except one tree.

What "work of the flesh" did Adam & Eve commit?

At the root: Disobedience. Scripture actually gives us a layered breakdown, not just one word. Genesis 3 + 1 John 2:16, the pattern in the Fall of Man lines up with the lust of the flesh, the lust of the eyes, and the pride of life." Lust of the Flesh: the devil convinced them that the fruit on this tree was *"Good for food" Adam and Eve had the d*esire to satisfy appetite, because they were not hungry. They weren't starving. Nowhere in Genesis does it say they were hungry. Unnecessary desire or appetite was stirred.

Lust of the Eyes: *"Pleasant to the eyes."* Attraction. Visual pull. "I want it because it looks good."

Pride of Life. *"Desired to make one wise"* "I want what God has not given me—BUT on my own terms." Well, these terms that have been presented, and they bought into the sales pitch.

So, what was the sin? **Disobedience** fueled by desire and pride. WAS IT GREED? Not greed in the financial sense. But I call it greed because they ate, and they weren't even hungry. They desired and they had no need. They wanted more…. That's **greed**.

They reached for something outside of what God had assigned. It wasn't greed for money, but unauthorized desire. The first loss in Scripture was not financial—it was the loss of position through disobedience.

Adam and Eve didn't lose money. They lost alignment, access, covering, and Structure. And once that was lost? Everything else followed. The works of the flesh don't just feel good—they **cost** you. They didn't need more—they stepped outside of order.

God gives, but when the flesh steps outside Structure, that's where loss begins.

Listening to the Serpent Adam and Eve lost paradise and was that not sorrow? The blessings of the Lord do not add sorrow with them.

In our day, works of the flesh such as unforgiveness are where people want to stay. Some are heard often saying, *I'll stay mad at them forever!* Happily, foolishly walking straight into bitterness and resentment. Forgiveness doesn't mean access. Go ahead and forgive them, before unforgiveness festers into something far worse. Then keep your distance.

People too often make revenge plans and plots… this is how the world behaves. You want to know what it's like to get revenge on someone when the Scripture clearly says venge is the Lord's? You're not God, but you want to do that? Then that is why God is not in your plans, maybe not in your money plans.

HOW NOT TO GET KINGDOMS

The first loss in Scripture did not seem like it was financial—it was the loss of position through disobedience." But how did it affect Adam and Eve from day to day? How did it affect their provision? Because before, they had everything, more than enough of everything. Then they were kicked out of the Garden and had to struggle just to grow food to eat.

Before Abraham and all his wealth, Before Solomon and all his riches, Adam and Eve lost the first empire of the Bible: The Garden of Eden… it doesn't say they owned it, but they had full access to everything in it except one tree.

Knowing what we know now, and having everything else except that TREE, we could walk past that tree every day for 100 years and never be tempted… couldn't we? Shouldn't we?

They didn't.

Adam and Eve traded the empire – the paradise they lived in. They didn't own it—but they had dominion, access, and provision." they lost it… because they stepped outside of order.

God did not remove provision. They removed themselves from the place where provision flowed. You don't lose money first. You lose order first when you step outside of order— you don't just lose what you have… you lose the **place** it flows from.

Looking at this evil irony: Adam and Eve essentially obeyed the Serpent and LOST the Garden of Eden (a kingdom of this world) then the devil turns around in the New Testament and tells Jesus if you worship me, I'll GIVE you kingdoms. WHAT A LIAR. Adam and Eve didn't know that, but Jesus did and now we do.

In Eden — Genesis 3. The serpent doesn't present himself as "worship me." He questions God's word, then offers a shortcut: You will be like God… (Gen 3:5)

Result: They obeyed another voice. They stepped outside God's order.

They lost dominion, access, and covering. The serpent didn't need them to worship him— he just needed them to believe him over God.

In the Wilderness — Matthew 4 / Luke 4, the devil is more direct:

All these kingdoms I will give you… if you worship me.
(Matt 4:9)

Jesus' response:

You shall worship the Lord your God, and Him only shall you serve. (Matthew 4:10)

The irony? The enemy tempts man, telling him that he will gain, but that victim ends up losing the very thing that causes loss.

- In Eden: *"Take this—gain more."* → they lose everything
- In the wilderness: *"Take this—gain kingdoms."* → Jesus refuses and keeps His position

IS THE DEVIL LYING? Well, yeah. He is: a liar (John 8:44) a tempter who distorts. But he doesn't always lie by fabricating— he lies by offering what is not his to give and demanding the wrong price.

Even if he claims "authority," it's limited and temporary. And whatever man receives, it is illegitimate when received through disobedience. Anything gained outside God's order cannot be kept <u>within</u> God's order.

The power to get wealth – we want wealth from god and God only because the power to keep that wealth will also come from GOD. Why do we need power to KEEP wealth? Because the enemy is coming for anything good that you get from God. Money, health, wealth, marriage, family, ministry, business, career… unless **God** is protecting you and what He gives you.

The devil will offer you what you lost—but only through the same disobedience that made you lose it.

So, don't venture out to gain by ungodly methods and then think God will help you keep it. Some try to get wealth through shortcuts, pressure, or compromise— but if it comes through disobedience, it won't stay through obedience.

If what a person gets comes through disobedience, it will take disobedience, violence and more sin to try to keep it. There is no guarantee that he will even keep it. God requires what a man stole from another every day of the week. Double for that innocent man's trouble all the way up to seven fold of what was stolen, even if it spoils that thief's house.

Gaining to hook or crook or by mischief and thievery is the plot of too many movies – one more heist, then we'll go straight after this. We'll make so many millions or billions and then we'll go straight after that—we'll be set for life.

It's not that God can't sanctify and make holy any money, but the entity that helped you get it? YOU OWE THEM…. What entity: IT TAKES POWER TO GET WEALTH IN THIS EARTH SYSTEM. So, will you use Godly power or corrupt power to get wealth?

If you get wealth by crooked means, don't then run knocking on the gates of Heaven to try to hide that thing you stole from so and so and ask God can you keep it there for a while until things blow over. Or, asking God to protect you FROM the sin—the method by how you got it, if it was not by God. You need to repent and get your gains from God, in Christ by His order.

In this way the one who gave you the POWER to get wealth will be the one to help you keep it and ENJOY IT. Enjoy the fruits of your labor.

In contrast to Jesus, Adam listened to the wrong voice. reached for what was offered then lost alignment and position.

Jesus modeled the right response: He refused the wrong voice, rejected the shortcut, and remained in position. Because He stayed in position.

What was promised came through the right order—not compromise. The enemy doesn't just tempt you to sin—he tempts you to secure through disobedience what God only sustains through order. That right there should tell a person the hinge of the devil's plan. If what he gives you cannot be kept, he can come by tomorrow and just take it back. Only what God gives is protected as long as you are in right order with God. Only what God protects can be kept from the devil. Nothing else is safe.

This is why we see, in or out of the movies, criminals who are just a bit nutso whacko, crazy, and even paranoid, because they are in great fear of losing what they have. When you get it from God, there is none of that emotional sorrow attached. When you get increase from ungodly means—well, a wicked man flees when no one is even chasing him. This is why this type in movies and in real life are surrounded with guards, security, and guns. They are protecting one of two things: Gain they got from other than God, or gain they got that they know is stolen, not theirs even if they don't know where it came from. Crooked gains gotten by crooked means, God is not protecting that.

In the movies, these people usually die for it or die protecting it. Hell awaits.

That's not any of us. Amen. We get our increase the right way, from God, in Christ and the Lord let's us enjoy the fruits of our increase.

The very cleverest of criminals believe that they have learned to mask their crookedness, their evil. They believe and too many are successful (for a time) that they are able to hide that and they are bold in public knowing that they are crooked in private. Don't worry, a man's ways will find him out. There are people with discernment, and God looks on the heart, not at the face of a man who is playacting.

Corrupt methods cost: money, access, time, relationships, stability. They could cost a man everything. Often, the cost is not paid all at once. It is paid over time. Repeatedly. Until YOU FINALLY NOTICE.

The question is not whether something feels right. The question is: What does it cost to first get it? Then, what will it cost to sustain it?

A person can gain access, opportunity, even influence— and still lose. Gain without Godly Structure becomes loss over time.

COST OF THE FLESH

Paying Without Realizing That You Are Paying

The Works of the Flesh:

Now the works of the flesh are manifest, which are *these*; Adultery, fornication, uncleanness, lasciviousness, Idolatry, witchcraft, hatred, variance, emulations, wrath, strife, seditions, heresies, Envyings, murders, drunkenness, revellings, and such like: of the which I tell you before, as I have also told *you* in time past, that they which do such things shall not inherit the kingdom of God. (Galatians 5:19–21)

Adultery / Sexual Immorality. Hidden spending is a hallmark of having side pieces and adultery. People start leading double lives--,one for their public image and another for their private secrets. Later, they will incur the egal costs of divorce, separation, separate dwelling places and child support, all leading to loss of stability.

How can I say this? Well, if the divorce rate is over 50 percent, ALL men, and ALL women are not cheating in their marriage. So, if only ½ of those who are married are cheaters then **ALL** the cheaters are getting caught and getting divorced. The other 50 percent are staying married.

In the process of that sin, what is gained? Temporary pleasure? What is lost? Structure, trust, and often wealth.

God multiplies in the context of marriage. Divorce is a divider.

Fornication. Like other works of the flesh, it promises fleeting satisfaction but exacts a hidden price. What is gained in a moment of pleasure is soon lost in the erosion of trust, the breakdown of Structure, and the slow draining of resources—both seen and unseen. The cost is not always paid upfront; often, it lingers, quietly undermining relationships, stability, and peace. Without Godly order, what appears to be gained is ultimately forfeited, and the soul pays more than it ever expected.

Impurity / Uncleanness. Undisciplined living. Poor decision-making. This causes financial leakage through lack of restraint. Cost: disorder that affects everything else.

Lasciviousness (lack of restraint). Impulse spending. Overindulgence through having no boundaries . The cost is the inability to hold anything long-term.

Idolatry

- Misplaced priorities
- Serving things instead of governing them
- Money flowing toward what controls you

Cost: you fund what rules you.

Witchcraft (manipulation, intimidation, domination, and or control). Trying to force outcomes. This leads a person to making bad deals and choices under pressure. They end up paying financially and spiritually for shortcuts that may not even work out. And even if they do, they are short lived because who will protect you from having those things stolen from you—even stolen by the same one who 'gave' them to you. The real cost is paying more to control what should be governed.

Hatred. Broken relationships. Lost opportunities. Isolation from networks. Cost: access denied.

Variance (constant conflict). Legal disputes. Business instability.

- Strained partnerships . Cost: money spent managing conflict.

Emulations (jealousy / comparison-itis). Keeping up with others. Overspending to match appearances. Cost: money spent on what was never assigned to you.

Wrath. Reactive decisions. Destroying opportunities in moments. Financial consequences of anger. Cost: decisions made in heat that must be paid for in time.

Strife is **c**onstant friction that creates unproductive environments. Loss of focus. Cost: energy and money drained by disorder. Seditions (division). Broken teams. Fragmented systems. Loss of collective strength . Cost: what could have been built together is lost apart.

Heresies (misaligned beliefs). Wrong thinking → wrong decisions. Investing in what does not hold. Cost: building on shifting ground.

Envy. Resentment-driven choices. Wanting what others have without Structure. Cost: pursuing outcomes you cannot sustain.

Murders (destruction). Not always physical, but it can be. It destroys relationships and sabotages opportunities. Cost: loss of what could have lived.

Drunkenness. Lack of control. Financial irresponsibility. Long-term instability. The cost: loss of governance. In many of these cases – loss of everything.

Revelings (excess / partying). Wasteful spending. No long-term return. Cost: money spent with nothing to show for it. Every work of the flesh does one of three things:

1. Distorts decision-making
2. Removes discipline
3. Redirects resources

once those are affected… Loss is inevitable. The flesh does not ask: "Can you afford this?" It asks: "Do you want this now?"

If Structure is not present, the answer is yes. It is always, yes. In this case, a person is not just losing money. They are funding what is ungoverned. They are funding what is actually working against them.

What a person may call gain may already be loss—if what they are gaining is costing you the ability to keep anything at all.

For what shall it profit a man, if he shall gain the whole world, and lose his own soul? Or what shall a man give in exchange for his soul? (Matthew 8: 36-37)

The world -- we are supposed to be in it but not of it. We are supposed to hate the world. The world… in the wilderness, the devil was trying to make Jesus trade His soul, For the kingdoms of this world.

The world? *Things and stuff?* Surely. But the world. To be able to do what the world does, party, drink, live any kinda way, wear any kinda thing… do what they do AND do God on Sunday – do what they do all week and then church, in the Kingdom, in the BODY on Sunday.

Worse, just in church long enough to get a blessing with intention to leave and do what you want after you get what you want from God. Nope. Can't do it; can't do both.

Here's a clue: if a person is trading with the devil—even if the person doesn't *look* like the devil, but by discernment they are talking like the devil, (an evil human agent) and the innocent person has nothing, no money, no wallet, nothing to 'trade' with, this is a spiritual transaction, not financial. Know this: Finances can be attached later, in addition to what the devil really wants.

So, Jesus is driven into the Wilderness after His baptism--, did he have money to trade with? No. If you have no money, especially if you've been driven into desperation, that's when the devil is most likely after your soul, although you shouldn't be trading with him anyway.

THE HOUSE AND THE BARN

Why More Storage Is Not Structure.

Not everything that holds is structured to sustain. A house and a barn both contain. But they are not the same. A house is ordered. It is designed for living, governance, protection, and continuity. A barn is for storage. It holds what is gathered. It holds what is accumulated. It holds what is not immediately used.

Both have purpose. But they are not usually interchangeable, notwithstanding those who build barndominiums. Most do not live in a barn, and most do not govern from it.

Some people are trying to solve structural problems by building barns. They are preparing, they think, for more accounts. They are creating more space, and more places to put what is coming in. Storage is not Structure. A barn can be full and still be disordered. Because what is stored is not necessarily governed.

THE ERROR is when increase comes, the instinct is often, "I need more room." So, more is built. More capacity to hold. More places to put. More accumulation. But nothing is corrected. No order. No discipline. No governance. So, what happens? The problem expands.

Because what was unstructured at one level remains unstructured at another.

GREED AND EXPANSION. There is a point where increase stops being stewardship and becomes accumulation. It becomes greed. It becomes hoarding. If it is not for use or purpose, but just to have more that's greed. We see this often in the grocery store when a storm is coming – where is all the toilet paper, really?

Greed does not always look excessive. Sometimes it looks like unexamined expansion. Building more without asking why. Storing more without structuring what is already there. It is adding without governing. Eventually what was meant to support begins to strain. Because more does not fix disorder. It multiplies it.

There is a wrong kind of money; every dollar is not a good dollar. Not all money strengthens Structure. Some money introduces instability. Money that comes without order, without discipline, without alignment and without assignment is usually not good money.

Increase that requires compromise, secrecy, or mismanagement is not good money; it is pressure. Sometimes it is a test – God is looking to see if you will take what is not yours or take what should not be taken. What enters your Structure must be carried by it. If it cannot be governed, it will destabilize what already exists. There is no Structure for money that violates order. It will not sit quietly. It will demand more, distort decisions, attract further disorder. And eventually, it will expose everything.

Being miserly and hoarding are both against **God's order.** Not all disorder is spending. Some disorder is withholding. Holding without purpose. Keeping without use. Accumulating without governance. This is not stewardship. It is fear.

A Structure that does not release becomes rigid. And rigidity is not strength. It is brittleness. What does not flow appropriately cannot function properly. Because Structure is not only about holding. It is about right movement.

THE REAL ISSUE. The problem is not how much you have, how much you store, how much you can accumulate. The problem is can what you have be governed? If not, more will not help. Another barn will not fix it.

THE WARNING, You can fill every space available and still have no structure. You can accumulate greatly and still lose. Because what is not governed is not secure.

You do not need more places to store what comes. You need a structure that knows what to do with it. (Luke 12:16–21)

The Man Who Built Bigger Barns. A certain man increased. His ground brought forth plentifully. And his response was not governance. It was expansion. I will pull down my barns, and build greater… He did not ask What is this for? What must be established? What must be governed? He asked: "Where do I put more?"

So, he built more storage, more capacity to hold. But nothing was ordered. No Structure. No governance. No accounting for what he could not carry. God's response was not about his wealth. It was about his **lack of Structure**

But God said unto him, Thou fool, this night thy soul shall be required of thee: then whose shall those things be, which thou hast provided (Luke 12:20)

Because he had increase without governance, accumulation without Structure, and storage without purpose. He built barns… But never built himself. That night, his life was required. Not because he had much. But because what he had was not structured to remain.

You can build bigger barns and still have nowhere for your life to stand.

Be made more empathetic, sympathetic so you don't become pathetic. Lord, light my path, in the Name of Jesus.

A person can acquire more space without acquiring more Structure. More than 155,000 storage units are auctioned off for abandonment, and nonpayment in this country alone per year. Storage units exist for the reason that people want to keep things that they are not using. Is it just in case they will use it or need it later? Or can they just not let go, even of things they can't govern? What cannot be managed at their house, a person may move out of sight to a storage unit. But even out of sight, that space must still be governed. It must be maintained. It must be paid for. It must be remembered.

And many are not. Instead, they are neglected, forgotten and eventually taken. I'll share a hard lesson I learned. Don't give your storage unit key to just anybody with instructions that they can go and get whatever the one or two things are that you are giving them without supervision or absolute knowledge that they are only taking what was given and nothing else. Even if that person is a close or long-time friend. Even if that person is a relative. Because when you go to your storage unit just three months later to close it out and move to your new apartment, you may find it has been raided and all your things have been given away or sold. That was many, many years ago for me, but I was not governing that storage unit.

More space does not solve disorder. It only delays the exposure of it.

While we are at it, no offense, ladies, but a purse fills up with all kinds of stuff, receipts, makeup, all kinds of items. These thing are added over time. Instead of removing what does not belong…another purse is acquired.

Not because more is needed, no, it is because what is already there has not been governed. You took out the stuff you were actually using, your wallet, driver's license and credit cards. Your house key and your favorite lipstick. The other stuff – ungoverned stuff.

More containers do not solve disorder; they conceal it.

This doesn't just apply to ladies' handbags. It applies to drawers and closets in your house. It applies to cars, phones and even storage units

A space fills. Not all at once, but things are added gradually. And instead of clearing what does not belong, another space is created. A new container. A new place to hold what has not been managed.

More space does not establish order. It extends what is already ungoverned.

A purse is replaced instead of cleared and that governance problem, corrected. Men? A new backpack or gym bag is added instead of emptying and organizing the old one. The same tool is purchased again because what was owned cannot be located. You're the king of that garage; where are the other three wrenches you bought last year?

This waste of time and money is not because there is no capacity. But it is because there is no order.

More space does not solve disorder; it conceals it.

When what cannot be found is repurchased—oh please. .

Disorder does not only waste space. It wastes money.

Can't deny it. Anyone who has moved from a house or place they lived in for five or more years knows what I'm talking about. Years pass. Items are added; old things ae rarely removed. Some are labeled as keepsakes.

Closets fill. Drawers fill. Rooms begin to hold what is no longer used. Because it happens gradually, it is not addressed--, until it is time to move.

Suddenly you can't believe you have all this stuff.

Time does not organize, It reveals what has not been.

- **Sun** → long exposure
- **Time/Pressure** → accumulation

- **Neglect** → not reviewing
- **Varmints** → small additions
- **Weight** → too much to manage

What is added slowly is often ignored completely.

You don't discover what you own as much as you discover what you've allowed.

What fills a house can also fill and crowd a life. Gradually. When it is not governed, it accumulates.

What you do not manage, over time, will eventually confront you all at once.

HOW TO KEEP MONEY

God gives the power to get wealth. Deuteronomy 8:18

How do you keep money?

This book has been all about building the house that can hold provision or building an entire ark system that can defend would-be attackers or your life, including money. We've talked about the dangers of having no Structure.

We can even consider that if you or your money are being attacked, maybe it's not even your fault. Well, you don't believe it is, but you have noticed that every time you take steps forward there's witches and evil agents (human and otherwise) coming at you to undo what progress you've made.

This could be ancestral. Generational. Familial.... All that could be true. Could be individual—your own sin, transgression and iniquity --- but prospering your soul means staying out of the flesh.

No matter what you inherited, if you have built a solid Structure that is secure, that gives the devil NO WAY IN, NO way to get to you, no way to attack you. NO way to steal, kill, or destroy. So, we all have to check ourselves. The Holy Spirit will bring us under conviction and show us the error of our own ways.

If you realize your money is being stolen, first get out of shock over the financial attack, and then figure out what is happening. Are you even *receiving* money or is the blockage upstream from there?

So, you are receiving; okay good. Where is it going? Is it being devoured, emptied, scattered, wasted, swallowed??? Then we must engage in warfare based on what evil forces have been sent in to steal. Seal up those access points.

We do not fail to repent for our ancestors and generations all the way back to Adam and Eve. Biblically, historically we will look at how others stewarded and we might get clues about our own ancestors. This will inform our prayer life and future decisions.

Adam and Eve did a not so good job of stewarding the Garden and got kicked out. Abraham seemed to have done a great job at owning money and kept it. Solomon? The Rich Young Ruler Owned money and it was sorrowful for him. Joseph was more prudent than his brothers; he was a very wise steward.

Adam & Eve basically failed at stewardship. They were given dominion, access, and provision to a rich and provisional paradise. They failed at obedience (self-governance). The result was a loss of place. They didn't lose money, *per se;* they lost the place that produced everything.

Abraham — Obedience + Alignment. Blessed with wealth. But key moment: willing to offer Isaac. Shows that nothing owned him. Abraham had another key moment when he gave; he gave ten percent of all his gain to Melchizedek. Abraham had wealth—but wealth did not have Abraham.

Solomon — Wealth + Drift. Given wisdom which produced wealth. Later: misalignment, divided heart. Result: wealth + sorrow / instability. A person can have Wisdom and still drift if alignment breaks.

The Rich Young Ruler fell into the ownership trap. Had wealth, but could not release it. Result: he walked away from the Jesus because what he owned… owned him. Go, sell what you have and give… that selfish greed, pride… were works of the flesh. Also if we think about it: JESUS GAVE A WORD AND THAT MAN DISOBEYED IT. So, add disobedience in there.

Of note, we don't know where the Rich Young Ruler got his wealth. When money is not gotten from God, it can have weird stipulations on it, such as, You can never give this money away. Or, You can never help the poor, or your relatives. If it is gotten from especially dark kingdoms, the instruction may be something like, You can never give to whomever you stole it from. Perhaps the Rich Young Ruler stole it from the poor…. The Bible doesn't say that; this is for thought.

Joseph was a true steward. He managed Potiphar's house. Prison, and eventually, Egypt. Joseph was faithful in every level. Result: he was entrusted with everything Joseph didn't ask for control—he proved he could be trusted.

Money doesn't stay where there is possession; it stays where there is stewardship, obedience, and alignment. Money is not lost first, the ability to govern, the authority to govern money is lost first.

Adam and Eve couldn't steward themselves in the Garden, therefore, they lost access to it. Abraham was blessed, but he stayed aligned, so it remained. Joseph stewarded everything—and God kept increasing him.

Solomon had wealth, but drifted, so sorrow entered. The rich young ruler had money, but couldn't release it, so he lost life. The man who built bigger barns. *Parable of the Rich Fool:* His land produced abundantly. He said: *"I'll tear down my barns and build bigger ones."* He planned to store, secure, and enjoy.

God said: Luke 12:20 *"Thou fool, this night thy soul shall be required of thee…"*

God is not looking for people who can get money to hold and hoard, He is looking for people who can be trusted with it. He treated provision like possession instead of stewardship. He said, *"my crops" "my barns" "my goods" "my soul"* . Everything was centered on himself. Did he ask God? Seems his entire purpose was not beyond himself. There was no stewardship mindset just ownership mindset. He built storage …but not stewardship. He planned for comfort …but not accountability. He secured resources …but ignored his soul

Ye have not because ye ask not or ye ask amiss (James) If it's just to heap on your own lust, this could be why God hasn't answered yet. God does give people money, but He releases far more to the one who will steward and not hoard or be stingy.

PERSON	ISSUE	RESULT
Adam & Eve	disobedience	lost place
Abraham	obedience	sustained blessing
Solomon	misalignment	sorrow
Rich Young Ruler	attachment	walked away
Joseph	stewardship	increase
Rich Fool	self-centered accumulation	life cut off

THE REAL WARNING:

Money that is kept without purpose will eventually expose what is missing. So, it's so much more than how to keep money, it's how to keep money flowing to you, so you can bless and be a blessing.

You don't keep money by storing it, although you should have some margins. You keep money by stewarding it under God. What belongs to Him, He protects. Who belongs to Him; He protects. What is dedicated to Him; He protects. You don't have to do it all alone out here in this world. Yes, you do take measures, you take steps in the Lord, but you are not alone trying to gather up and hoard great hoards of money.

The following section is not the end of this book. It is simply a personal checkpoint, a place to stop and notice what is already present in your Structure.

What you glean from it will establish what must be aligned.

DIAGNOSTIC CHECKLIST

Where Is It Going—and Why? Be honest with yourself.

SECTION 1 — STRUCTURE

Do you have order, or are you relying on awareness?

- ☐ I consistently track where my money goes
- ☐ I review patterns, not just balances
- ☐ I correct small leaks quickly
- ☐ I have clear boundaries on spending
- ☐ My decisions are intentional, not reactive

If multiple are unchecked:
You are not lacking money. You are lacking Structure.

SECTION 2 — VARMINTS (SMALL LEAKS)

Where is money leaving in small, repeated ways?

- ☐ Subscriptions or charges I don't review
- ☐ Frequent "small" purchases I don't track
- ☐ Impulse spending justified as minor
- ☐ Repeated financial habits I haven't questioned

If yes:
You are being drained quietly, not attacked directly.

SECTION 3 — MOISTURE (INTERNAL COMPROMISE)

Where have your standards shifted?

- ☐ I justify decisions I used to avoid
- ☐ I make emotional financial choices
- ☐ I say “it’s not that serious” often
- ☐ I delay correcting what I know is off

If yes:
Your Structure is being softened from within.

SECTION 4 — NEGLECT

What have you not checked?

- ☐ Accounts I haven’t reviewed
- ☐ Patterns I’ve ignored
- ☐ Habits I’ve allowed to continue
- ☐ Systems I’ve stopped maintaining

If yes:
Loss is already in motion—it just hasn’t shown fully yet.

SECTION 5 — WEIGHT

What are you carrying that you never structured for?

- ☐ Increased income without changed discipline
- ☐ More responsibility without better systems
- ☐ Too many people influencing financial decisions
- ☐ People with access who are not governed

If yes:
You are not failing—you are overloaded.

SECTION 6 — FIRE (INCREASE)

What happened when more came?

- ☐ Spending increased with income
- ☐ Discipline did not increase with opportunity
- ☐ Access expanded without boundaries
- ☐ Decisions became faster, not wiser

If yes:
Increase exposed your Structure —it did not fix it.

SECTION 7 — WIND (INFLUENCE)

What is moving your decisions?

- ☐ Other people's opinions
- ☐ Social comparison

- ☐ Trends or urgency
- ☐ Emotional pressure

If yes:
You are being influenced, not governed.

SECTION 8 — COLD (SCARCITY RESPONSE)

What happens when things tighten?

- ☐ I panic or restrict excessively
- ☐ I make fear-based decisions
- ☐ I lose consistency in discipline
- ☐ My Structure disappears under pressure

If yes:
Your order is conditional, not established.

SECTION 9 — SUN (LONG EXPOSURE)

What have you stopped paying attention to because "things are fine"?

- ☐ I no longer review what used to matter
- ☐ I assume things will continue working
- ☐ I have not adjusted systems over time
- ☐ I operate on autopilot

If yes:
You are being worn down by what you are not maintaining.

SECTION 10 — TIME / PRESSURE

What has been building?

- ☐ Repeated small losses
- ☐ Patterns I've allowed to continue
- ☐ Decisions I keep making the same way
- ☐ Issues I've delayed addressing

If yes:
You are experiencing accumulation, not randomness.

FINAL DIAGNOSIS

You are not dealing with isolated issues.
You are dealing with a Structure under multiple forces.

**Where you checked the most boxes—
that is where your Structure is weakest.**

What you correct first
will determine what you are able to keep next.

CHECK YOURSELF

What Are You Funding That Works Against You?

What you repeatedly choose you repeatedly pay for. **Ask Directly: What am I doing that does not promote keeping what I receive?**

WILLFUL COSTS

Be honest.

- ☐ Spending to sustain habits I know are harmful
- ☐ Paying for temporary relief (food, shopping, substances, distractions)
- ☐ Funding environments that drain me
- ☐ Repeating choices that consistently cost me money
- ☐ Ignoring the financial impact of my behavior

SUBSTANCES / ESCAPES

- ☐ Alcohol I regularly purchase
- ☐ Substances that require ongoing money
- ☐ "Recreation" that leaves no return
- ☐ Spending to maintain an escape, not a life

Ask:
Who can afford this repeatedly?
What else could this money have sustained?

IMPULSE & JUSTIFICATION

- ☐ Buying what I didn't plan
- ☐ Using money to regulate emotion
- ☐ Saying "I deserve this" without Structure
- ☐ Calling it small when it is consistent

PATTERNED LOSS

- ☐ The same type of spending over and over
- ☐ The same consequences over and over
- ☐ The same regret over and over

This is not random. This is **established behavior**.

THE REAL COST

The wages of sin is death—
but before that, there is cost.

It costs money on the front end, money on the back end, and if it can be sustained at all, it will take money to sustain it. If that weren't enough, it will take money to recover from it. Some pay to enter. Some pay to maintain. Some pay to get out. Most pay all three.

HARD QUESTIONS

- What am I funding that is weakening me?
- What am I paying for that produces no return?
- What am I sustaining that is unsustainable?
- What would change if I stopped paying for this?

TRUTH

You cannot build Structure while financing disorder. You cannot keep money while spending against your own stability. You are not just losing money. You are paying for what is working against you.

Who can afford to keep paying for what destroys them?

STILL CHECKING:

Not all loss is hidden. Some of them are chosen. Not everything leaving your life is being taken. Some of it is being funded. I know a woman who justifies gambling and losses at gambling as, “That’s just the cost of entertainment, and that is my entertainment.” Yet she complains about not having money, a lot.

The works of the flesh are not only spiritual issues. They are financial decisions. They require: money, time, access, and maintenance.

The wages of sin is death. But before that, there is cost.

You pay to enter, to sustain, to recover. But can any of us **afford what all that is costing?**

Who can afford ongoing substance habits?

Who can afford chronic emotional spending?

Who can afford repeated impulsive decisions?

Who can afford environments that require you to keep paying to stay in them?

Whatever any of us do that does not promote keeping resources is working against us. Who can build stability while financing instability?

In that case the person is not just losing money, they are paying for what is undoing them.

THE STANDARD

What Ultimately Holds

When the enemy shall come in like a flood,
the Spirit of the Lord shall lift up a standard against him.
(Isaiah 59:19)

The flood is coming in, but what are you going to do about it when it does? The verse says that God is going to do something about it; so pray and put your faith in God who will lift up a Standard against this flood..

What is the Standard?

Lifting up a Standard doesn't mean that God will make a bigger flood. In ancient warfare, when a Standard was a raised banner or flag. It signaled who ruled the field, where authority stood, where order had been established. Jehovah Nissi: the Lord My Banner.

The Standard was not the battle; it was what held position during the battle. The flood of the enemy and the Standard are not the same thing; they are opposites.

Being opposites, a flood is pressure and chaos, force and sudden movement. Whereas a Standard is Structure, order, alignment, and authority. When the flood rises, something must already exist that does not move with it.

The Standard is that thing.

The Standard is Structure. It is something established before pressure arrives. And in response to the flood God lifts it up even higher. The Standard is truth in place. It is established discipline. It is boundaries set, governance active, and order maintained.

The Ark and the Standard. The ark was not built during the flood. It was built before the flood. It was built while nothing appeared wrong. While others continued business as usual, thinking the sun would always shine and that it would not ever smite them. While there was no visible pressure, a man built an ark because he was aligned with God.

The ark was Structure established in advance. And when the flood came. The ark did not stop the water, but it did preserved what was placed within it.

The Invisible Architecture: Every life has Structure. Even if it is not recognized. People see outcomes, stability, provision, and peace. But what holds up those things? It is the unseen that brings to bear the things which are seen. What holds those things up is rarely seen.

Structure is not the visible result. It is the invisible framework. Discipline, Wisdom. It is order, priorities, boundaries, and governance.

These do not draw attention except sometimes to make the person operating in them look boring, predictable. To God, that man looks diligent and stable, but to a carnal man he looks mundane. Yet, these are the things that determine everything.

Many attempt to fix visible problems without addressing invisible Structure. In this way they are reaching to correct symptoms without fixing the real issue. In his reach he may blame circumstances, opposition, and external pressure. All those things may exist. All those things may be sure to exist. How do I know that? My Bible tells me so.

Many are the afflictions of the righteous: but the Lord delivereth him out of them all. (Psalm 34:19)

Sometimes the issue is not the flood. Although we should not embrace the flood, it has come to show us weaknesses in our Structure, chinks in our armor, holes in the fabric of our pockets.

Sometimes the issue is nothing was built, or the wrong thing was built to withstand it.

Structure functions like an ark, keeping in what must be preserved and keeping out what must not enter. Keeping alive what must be kept alive; Noah's ark did that. Joseph did that when he said, "I've come to save many people alive." The ark of the Covenant did that when it went before the people into battles; then they were victorious. Jesus did that; redeeming us all from sin and death.

But as for you, ye thought evil against me; but God meant it unto good, to bring to pass, as it is this day, to save much people alive. (Genesis 50:20)

The ark holds provision, stability, peace, and what has been entrusted.

It resists disorder, waste, destruction, and ungoverned access. This dual function is not optional. Without it, nothing remains contained.

The Standard is not always visible. It shows up as Truth where deception once was. It shows up as discipline where there was disorder. It is Wisdom where there was impulse. The Standard is governance where there was drift.

It is steady. Because it is steady… The flood loses power. Ultimately, the flood does not stop because it weakens; it stops because it meets something stronger.

As discussed, the flood will come in in different forms: pressure, increase, opportunity, or disruption. When it does, the question remains unchanged: Is there a Structure in place that can hold what arrives?

What is not established beforehand will not be formed in the moment. Before Abraham was, I AM. What is not structured will not remain. Before every flood, Jesus already WAS. He is the same yesterday, today, and forever.

The Spirit of the Lord raises a Standard. That standard is the order of God established in a life. Where that order is established…what should remain, remains.

The flood tests what has been built. The Standard reveals what stands.

When the enemy shall come in like a flood, the Spirit of the Lord shall lift up a standard against him. (Isaiah 59:19)

A standard marked the field. It it rallied the army. It signaled where order and authority were established. So, when Scripture says the Spirit of the Lord raises a

Standard, it means God establishes authority and order that pushes the flood back. The Standard is order even in the midst of chaos.

The flood is chaos, pressure, destruction.

The Standard is Structure, authority, and alignment,

In other words, when the flood comes, God raises something stronger than the flood. That "something" is the **order** of His kingdom.

Not all floods are the same. We've talked about three types that the enemy might send. But, not every flood has the same source. Not every flood has the same purpose. Not every flood requires the same response.

Recall, the enemy's flood is *to overwhelm, scatter, and destabilize.* This flood is sudden with no notice at all. It is aggressive and disorienting

It looks like pressure all at once. It looks like confusion, loss of clarity. Things start moving faster than they can be governed. Its goal is disorder and chaos. It's goal is, disorientation to render its victim confused and helpless if possible. Its goal is to overwhelm. It attempts to scatter focus, break Structure, and force reaction instead of governance.

What stops it? Not panic. Not reaction, or desperation or desire, but no, the Standard that the Lord raises will stop it. Order, already established, Structure already in place is what will stop it.

The enemy's flood loses power when it meets something that does not move, something it cannot move.

God has authority over all of Creation, including the waters. God's flood is what we see in the story of Noah's Ark.

To reset, cleanse, and judge

The flood in Noah's day was not chaotic; It was intentional. It came in measure over 40 days and nights, with instruction beforehand. With preservation already prepared. This flood removed what was corrupt. It preserved what was aligned, reset what had become disordered.

It was not random; it was judgment with reservation.

What mattered?

Not stopping the flood, but being in the ark. Because in this case, the flood was not the enemy. The flood was the instrument of correction. Everything obeys God; so if God said there would be constant rains for a period and also a flood; that is what would be.

The ark determined what survived, what remained, what continued forward.

THE HOUSE AS AN ARK

When Judgment Passes Through

Moving from Genesis to Exodus we see Creation still obeying God. Yet, not every flood is water. Some floods are events. Some are sequences. Some are consequences as Pharaoh would find out. Some move through a land instead of over it.

The plagues in Egypt came one after another. They were not random. They were measured, directed, purposeful. Each one struck a system. Each one exposed what could not stand. In that sense, they were floods. Not of water, but of judgment.

The final plague was different from the first nine. The 10tth moved to every house. The instruction was not to fight it, stop it, or escape it. The instruction came before the Plague, and it was, "Prepare the house." It was, "Mark the door." It was, "Stay inside. Remain where you have been placed." In today's terms, "Shelter in place."

In the 10th Egyptian plague, for the Hebrews, God's people, their house became an ark. That night, every marked house, sealed by the blood on the doorposts and lintel functioned as an ark for those inside. This was not because of its walls, but because of obedience, alignment, instruction followed.

Inside, life was preserved. Outside, loss occurred. The difference was not geography. It was what had been established at the door. Protection was in placement. They were told, Do not go out. Do not wander. Do not step beyond what has been marked. This mark was the seal, it was the sign, it was the Standard.

Once outside the Structure there was no covering. Structure is not always visible. But it determines what is preserved, what is lost, what passes through, and what does not.

That night proved Not every house is an ark. Only the house that is aligned and marked and sealed by the blood of the lamb. In the day of the Lord's judgment, in the day of His fury, people will not find a place to hide themselves.

And they shall go into the holes of the rocks, and into the caves of the earth, for fear of the Lord, and for the glory of his majesty, when he ariseth to shake terribly the earth.

To go into the clefts of the rocks, and into the tops of the ragged rocks, for fear of the Lord, and for the glory of his majesty, when he ariseth to shake terribly the earth. (Isaiah 2:19-21, see also revelations 6:14-17)

Some tried to survive by location. Others survived by instruction. The flood did not ask who was comfortable. It revealed: When judgment moves through a place, when everything that can be shaken, will be shaken, but only what has been properly marked is preserved.

The instruction was simple, "Stay in the house," not because the house itself was special. But because it had been prepared, it had been marked, it had been aligned. And so was the ark of Noah who was particular to stay in the ark until the test dove did not return. At that time Noah knew that the dove had found a place to alight and so the waters had abated and he and his family and all the animals could disembark the vessel of their safety and salvation from that great flood.

That night in Egypt, for the Hebrews who had marked and sealed doors, their house became an ark because it was brought into the Lord's order.

When the flood is not meant to be stopped, but still survived, God's order and His Standard will prevail, every time.

We see from the Ten Plagues that floods are not always water We see God prepares and provides vessels to save His people; an ark is not always a boat. We see Structure can be likened sometimes a house under instruction.

It is not the event that determines survival. It is the Structure in place when the event arrives.

The mark on the houses of the chosen and obedient on the night of the Passover, the houses were not preserved randomly. They were marked and sealed, as it were, by the blood of the lamb. The instruction was specific: Mark the door. Remain inside. Do not step outside what has been covered.

The mark did not change the Structure of the house physically, but it did establish alignment, covering, authority at the entry point. The difference was not the house itself. It was what had been applied to it.

This is the principle: It is not enough to have a Structure. The Structure must be properly marked.

Because that night proved unmarked houses were not preserved. Uncovered spaces were not protected. Unaligned Structures did not stand.

Structure is needed; it is necessary, but Structure alone is not enough. There must be alignment. Instruction must be followed. There must be proper covering, because a Structure without alignment cannot withstand what is passing through.

That night, some had houses. Some had houses that were marked. That was the difference. The flood did not decide what was taken; the mark did. The mark is the Standard.

That night, every marked house became an ark. Not because of what it looked like, and not because it was floating on water. But because it was covered, it was aligned, and it remained within instruction. The blood of the lamb marked the boundary between what was preserved and what was not.

Then, later all those who were within those marked houses walked free on dry land through the Red Sea. Noah and all that were in the ark he had built by the Lord's instruction were also on dry footing the entire time the floods raged outside the ark that Noah built, that the Lord had shut and sealed. This is no coincidence.

When judgment passes through, it does not respond to appearance. It responds to what has been established.

THE MARK AND THE STANDARD

On the night of the Passover, the houses were marked by the blood of the lamb. That mark was not decoration. It was not symbolic alone. It was a standard.

The Standard was seen at the door. The blood was applied at the entry point. It was not inside the house; it was not hidden, but at the boundary. The issue was not what was within, the issue was what was allowed to pass through. The mark was the standard; it established alignment, authority, and covering.

Structure is not only internal. It must also be established at the boundaries. It must be applied where entry is possible, at vulnerable access points to govern what comes in and what does not.

That night, the standard was not raised in the air, like a flag, it was applied at the door.

...and God shut the door of Noah's ark (Genesis 7:16 paraphrased)

The instruction was simple: Apply the blood. Remain inside. Do not cross the boundary. At that moment: The house became an ark because the standard had been established. And God shut the doors of those marked houses that night. God shut the lion's mouths for Daniel. God shuts doors that no man can open (Revelations).

The blood of the lamb was not only covering, it was the standard and the seal that determined what remained.

Stand up! stand up for Jesus! Ye soldiers of the cross; Lift high His royal banner, It must not suffer loss: From vict'ry unto vict'ry His army shall He lead, Till every foe is vanquished And Christ is Lord indeed. Stand up for Jesus Ye soldiers of the cross; Lift high His royal banner, It must not, it must not suffer loss.

Raise the Standard —and do not let it drop. The Standard must not suffer loss.

A banner in war marks territory, signals authority, shows who governs the field. So, when it says "*Lift high His royal banner*" It's saying, Establish the Standard where it can be seen and held.

Hold it. Don't let it drop.

That's not coincidence; that's alignment.

THE CARPENTER'S SON

The Romans were builders. They constructed roads, columns, and systems that carried weight and endured time. They understood measurement, alignment, and load. What they built was visible, engineered, and structured.

The One they crucified was the carpenter's Son. A carpenter understands what holds and what fails. A carpenter knows that if a beam is not set correctly, the entire structure is compromised. He knows that alignment is not decorative, it is essential. He knows that a structure does not collapse all at once, but fails at the point where something was not set, reinforced, or maintained.

This was neither incidental nor accidental.

The One placed on that Cross understood Structure at the most fundamental level. He understood alignment. He understood load. He understood what it takes for something to remain. The vertical beam must be plumb. The horizontal beam must be set correctly. If either is off, what is built cannot hold. Everything depends on alignment.

The Cross was not random wood assembled without thought. It was a Structure. A vertical beam and a cross beam, set in place. What the Romans constructed as an instrument of death became something far greater than they understood.

They built it., but Jesus defined it.

The vertical beam represents alignment with God. It is what is set straight, measured, and true. It determines whether anything built upon it can stand. If the vertical is off, nothing else can be corrected enough to compensate for it. The horizontal beam of Jesus' Cross on Golgotha represented what functions in the Earth. It is where connection happens, where relationships are formed, where outcomes are produced. But the horizontal cannot carry weight if the vertical is not established.

This is where many attempt to work. They adjust the horizontal. They try to fix what is around them—relationships, outcomes, environments—without addressing what is above them, addressing their relationship with God. They reinforce what is visible without correcting what is foundational.

Jesus, the Carpenter's Son was placed on a structure that required perfect alignment. Through that, something was restored that had been disrupted from the beginning. The Cross did not introduce something new; it restored what had been lost.

The Carpenter's Son did not simply die on that structure. He fulfilled it. He embodied it. He established a pattern of alignment that reconnected what had been separated.

The vertical was restored. Because of that, the horizontal could function again. This is structural. If the vertical is not aligned, the horizontal will always require strain. Things will not hold. Outcomes will not remain. What is built will have to be rebuilt, again and again, because the foundation is not set.

But when the vertical is established, the horizontal can carry weight. What is built can remain. What is produced can be sustained. This is about position. It is about whether what is foundational has been set correctly.

Again, once the vertical is established, everything else can be measured against it. Everything else can be corrected. Everything else can be brought into alignment.

If the vertical is ignored, nothing else will remain stable. The Romans built the Cross. The Carpenter's Son defined it. The vertical beam, and the cross beam: Jesus was the Beam on the Cross; the Light of the World, the plumbline, setting mankind right with God again.

WHAT WILL YOU ESTABLISH?

Nothing leaves randomly. What remains and what does not is determined by Structure.

In this book, by now, you have seen what moves against you, what enters quietly, what spreads within, what accumulates over time, what increase requires, what you may be funding yourself. You cannot unknow this. From this point forward, loss is no longer mysterious.

You will see where things are leaking, where things are softening, where things are ungoverned, where things are overloaded. The question will no longer be: "Why is this happening?" The question will be: *What have I not established?* Structure is not built in a moment. It is built in repeated, governed, and corrected and consistent decisions.

You do not need more money to begin. You need order, discipline, boundaries, and correction. What you correct will begin to hold. What you ignore will continue to leak. What you remove will stop draining. What you establish will remain. There is no Structure without authority.

You must decide what is allowed, what is not, what stays, and what goes. This is not done emotionally but objectively and permanently for your own good and to the Glory of God. Then ask the Lord to establish it in your life.

Some things will need to be cut off. Some patterns will need to end. Some access will need to be removed. Not because you cannot afford them but because they cost too much. No one can really afford to keep paying for what is ruining them.

You are not building for a moment. You are building for continuity, for what stays, for what holds, and for what does not collapse under pressure.

You will keep what your Structure can carry. So, establish it. Not later. Not when more comes. Now. Because what you build now will determine what you are able to keep when increase arrives. What you are unwilling to govern you will eventually lose.

THE END

I seal these words decrees, declarations and prayers across every dimension and timeline, past, present, and future, to infinity, in the Name of Jesus.

I seal them with the Blood of Jesus and the Holy Spirit of Promise.

Any retaliation against this author, the reader or anyone who prays these prayers, makes these decrees and declarations at any time, let that retaliation backfire on the head of the perpetrator to infinity, and without Mercy, in the Name of Jesus.

Dear Reader

Thank you for acquiring and reading this book, I pray it has blessed you to even more begin and live with the desired outcome in mind. But live, build Structure and be a wise steward in all things, to the Glory of God.

Shalom,

Dr. Marlene Miles

If you enjoyed this book, here are some new releases

Christ of God (*The*) 3-book series

Christ of God, (*The*) Box Set, includes all 3books

Other books on Authority:

These books were mentioned often in this one. They have many prayer points against the elite spiritual thieves:

The Emptiers https://a.co/d/heio0dO

The Wasters https://a.co/d/5TG1iNQ

The Swallowers https://a.co/d/1jWhM6G

The Devourers: Why We Can't Have Nice Things https://a.co/d/87Tejbf

Spiritual Thieves https://a.co/d/eqPPz33

Prayerbooks by this author

There are some books that are only prayers. You just open up the book and pray.

Prayers Against Barrenness: *For Success in Business and Life*

Fruit of the Womb: *Prayers Against Barrenness*

Beauty Curses, *Warfare Prayers Against*
https://a.co/d/5Xlc2OM

Courts of Marriage: Prayers for Marriage in the Courts of Heaven *(prayerbook)* https://a.co/d/cNAdgAq

Courtroom Warfare @ Midnight *(prayerbook)*
https://a.co/d/5fc7Qdp

Demonic Cobwebs *(prayerbook)* https://a.co/d/fp9Oa2H

Every Evil Bird https://a.co/d/hF1kh1O

Gates of Thanksgiving

Spirits of Death, Hell & the Grave, Pass Over Me and My House

Throne of Grace: Courtroom Prayer

Warfare Prayer Against Poverty
https://a.co/d/bZ61lYu

FAKE FRIENDS: *Prayers Against Betrayers*

HOLIDAY WARFARE Prayer Manual (humorous) Surviving Family Gatherings All Year Long (without catching a case)

SOUL TIE Prayer Manual (The) Part of a 3-part series including a workbook.

MAD at DADDY Prayer Manual – part of a 3-part series including a workbook.

Healing the Sibling & Relative Wound Prayer Manual

Healing the Father-Son Wound Prayer Manual

Breaking Curses of the Mother Prayer Manual

Other books by this author

Abundance of Jesus (The) https://a.co/d/5gHJVed

AK: The Adventures of the Agape Kid

Already Married in the Spirit: *Why You May Not Be Married in the Natural*

AMONG SOME THIEVES https://a.co/d/dkYT4ZV

Ancestral Powers

Anti-Marriage, *The Spirit of*

Backstabbers https://a.co/d/gi8iBxf

Barrenness, *Prayers Against* https://a.co/d/feUltIs

Battlefield of Marriage, *The*

Beware of the Dog: Prayers Against Dogs in the Dream.

Bless Your Food: *Let the Dining Table be Undefiled* *https://a.co/d/6oPMRDv*

Blindsided: *Has the Old Man Bewitched You?* https://a.co/d/5O2fLLR

Break Free from Collective Captivity

Broken Spirits & Dry Bones

By Means of a Whorish Father

Caged Life: Get Out Alive! https://a.co/d/bwPbksX

Casting Down Imaginations

Christ of God (*The*) 3-book series

Christ of God, (*The*) Box Set, includes all three books

Churchzilla, The Wanna-Be, Supposed-to-be Bride of Christ https://a.co/d/eAf5j3x

Collateral Damage: *When What Happened Spiritually Was Your Fault*

Demonic Cobwebs (prayerbook)

Demonic Time Bombs

Demons Hate Questions

Devil Loves Trauma, *The*

Devil Weapons: Unforgiveness, Bitterness,...

The Devourers: Thieves of Darkness 2

Do Not Swear by the Moon

Don't Refuse Me, Lord (4 book series)

https://a.co/d/idP34LG

Dream Defilement

The Emptiers: *Thieves of Darkness, 1*
https://a.co/d/5I4n5mc

Entanglements: Illegal Knots Limiting Your Life

Evil Touch

Failed Assignment

Fantasy Spirit Spouse https://a.co/d/hW7oYbX

FAT Demons (The): *Breaking Demonic Curses*
https://a.co/d/4kP8wV1

The Fold (5-book series)

- The Fold (Book 1)
- Name Your Seed (Book 2)
- The Poor Attitudes of Money (3)
- Do Not Orphan Your Seed (4)
- For the Sake of the Gospel (5)
- My Sowing Journal

Gang Ups: Touch Not God's Anointed

Gathered: No Longer Scattered
https://a.co/d/1i5DPIX

Getting Rid of Evil Spiritual Food

https://a.co/d/i2L3WYQ

got HEALING? Verses for Life

got LOVE? Verses for Life https://a.co/d/8seXHPd

got HOPE? Verses for Life

got money? https://a.co/d/g2av41N

Has My Soul Been Sold? https://a.co/d/dyB8hhA

Here Come the Horns: *Skilled to Destroy* https://a.co/d/cZiNnkP

Hidden Sins: Hidden Iniquity

https://a.co/d/4Mth0wa

How to Dental Assist

How to Dental Assist2: Be Productive, Not Wasteful

How To Stay Prayed Up

How to STOP Being a Blind Witch or Warlock

I Take It Back

In Multiplying I Will Multiply Thee

Into Freedom:

Irresistible: Jesus' Triumphal Entry
https://a.co/d/d09IfEC

KNOW YOUR BATTLE: Stop Swinging Blindly — and Win Against Opponents, Adversaries & Enemies (Workbook) https://a.co/d/eOwFKlV

Legacy

Let Me Have A Dollar's Worth
https://a.co/d/h8F8XgE

Level the Playing Field

Living for the NOW of God https://a.co/d/6bK5duE

Lose My Location https://a.co/d/crD6mV9

Love Breaks Your Heart

Mad At Daddy: Healing Father-Wounds that Affect Motherhood (book, workbook & prayer manual)

Made Perfect In Love

Mammon https://a.co/d/29yhMG7

Man Safari, *The*

Marriage Ed.: *Rules of Engagement & Marriage*

Made Perfect in Love

Money Hunters: Beware of Those

Money on the Altar https://a.co/d/4EqJ2Nr

Mulberry Tree, *The* https://a.co/d/9nR9rRb

Motherboard (The)- *Soul Prosperity Series*

Name Your Seed

Occupy: *Until I Return* https://a.co/d/bZ7ztUy

One Defining Day*: A Day When Dreams Come True*

Opponent, Adversary, or Enemy?: Fight The Right Battle with the Right Weapons

https://a.co/d/byQqEE2 & companion workbook: Know Your Battle

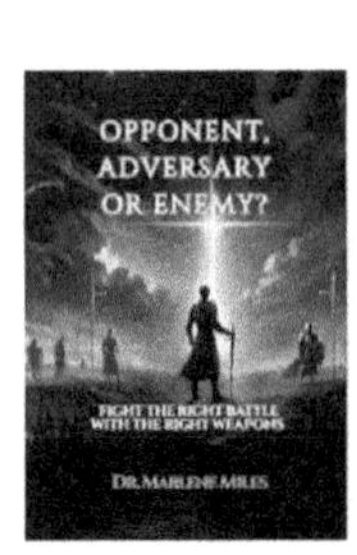

Plantation Souls

Players Gonna Play

<u>PLEAD YOUR CASE</u> book & Study Guide

Portals: Shut the Front Door: Prayers to Close Evil Portals.

Power Money: Nine Times the Tithe

https://a.co/d/gRt41gy

The Power to Get Wealth https://a.co/d/e4ub4Ov

Powers Above

The Robe, Part 1, The Lessons of Joseph

The Robe, Part II, The Lessons of Joseph

Seasons of Grief

Seasons of Siege: God Is Coming

Seasons of Waiting

Seasons of War

Second Marriage, Third--, *Any Marriage*

https://a.co/d/6m6GN4N

Seducing Spirits: Idolatry & Whoredoms

https://a.co/d/4Jq4WEs

Shut the Front Door: *Prayers to Close Portals*
https://a.co/d/cH4TWJj

Siege: *God Is Coming*

Sift You Like Wheat

The Silences of God:

Six Men Short: What Has Happened to all the Men?

SLAVE

Sleep Afflictions & Really Bad Dreams
https://a.co/d/f8sDmgv

Soul Prosperity soul prosperity series 3

https://a.co/d/5p8YvCN

Soul Ties: How Soul Ties Form, and How To Break Them (book, workbook & prayer manual)

Souls In Captivity

The Spirit of Anti-Marriage

The Spirit of Poverty https://a.co/d/abV2o2e

Spiritual Thieves https://a.co/d/eqPPz33

StarStruck- Triangular Power series.

SUNBLOCK- Triangular Power series.

The Swallowers: *Thieves of Darkness*, 3

Take It Back

This Is NOT That: How to Keep Demons from Coming at You

Thrones

Time Is of the Essence

Too Many Wives: *Why You Have Lady Problems*

Tormenting Spirits https://a.co/d/dAogEJf

Toxic Souls

Triangular Power *(series),* Powers Above, SUNBLOCK, Do Not Swear by the Moon, STARSTRUCK

TRIBE: *What Covenants Are Governing You…?*

Unbreak My Heart: *Don't Let Me Die*

Uncontested Doom

Ungovered Hunger: How Unchecked Appetite Dismantles Authority

Unguarded Hours, *The*

Unseen Life, *The* (forthcoming)

Upgrade: How to Get Out of Survival Mode Toxic Souls (Book 2 of series) , Legacy (Book 3 of series)

The Wasters: *Thieves of Darkness,* Bk 2 https://a.co/d/bUvI9Jo

What Have You to Declare? What Do You Have With You from Where You've Been?

When I Was A Child, *I Prayed As a Child*

When the Devourer is Rebuked https://a.co/d/1HVv8oq

When The Table Is Set Against You

WTH? Get Me Out of This Hell https://a.co/d/a7WBGJh

The Wilderness Romance ***(series)*** This series is about conducting a Godly relationship and marriage with someone who is a Wilderness person. ***The Social Wilderness***

- ***The Sexual Wilderness***
- ***The Spiritual Wilderness***

Other Series

The Fold (a series on Godly finances)

https://a.co/d/4hz3unj

Soul Prosperity Series https://a.co/d/bz2M42q

Spirit Spouse books

https://a.co/d/9VehDSo

https://a.co/d/97sKOwm

Battlefield of Marriage, The

https://a.co/d/eUDzizO

Players Gonna Play

https://a.co/d/2hzGw3N

Sent Spirit Spouse (can someone send you a spirit spouse? This book is not yet released.)

Matters of the Heart, Made Perfect in Love https://a.co/d/70MQW3O , Love Breaks Your Heart https://a.co/d/4KvuQLZ, Unbreak My Heart https://a.co/d/84ceZ6M Broken Spirits & Dry Bones https://a.co/d/e6iedNP

Thieves of Darkness series

The Emptiers https://a.co/d/heioOdO

The Wasters https://a.co/d/5TG1iNQ

The Swallowers https://a.co/d/1jWhM6G

The Devourers: Why We Can't Have Nice Things https://a.co/d/87Tejbf

Spiritual Thieves

Red Flags: The Track Is Not Safe (book & workbook)

Triangular Powers https://a.co/d/aUCjAWC

Upgrade (series) *How to Get Out of Survival Mode* https://a.co/d/aTERhX0

We Get Along, Right? Compatibility for Couples – (book & workbook)

Dr. Marlene Miles is a teacher, author, and spiritual thinker known for her grounded, discerning approach to prayer and spiritual formation. Her work emphasizes clarity, restraint, and maturity in faith—helping believers move beyond emotionalism and performance into a steady, practiced walk with God.

With a deep respect for Scripture and a practical understanding of daily life, Dr. Miles writes for those who want their prayer life to be formed, not dramatized. Her teaching encourages spiritual maintenance, discernment, and responsibility—so faith remains strong not only in crisis, but in everyday living.

www.ingramcontent.com/pod-product-compliance
Lightning Source LLC
LaVergne TN
LVHW010946110826
845149LV00015B/3228

9781971933498